Wicked
MACON

Wicked MACON

Sinners & Saints in the Heart of Georgia

Phillip Andrew Gibbs

THE
History
PRESS

Published by The History Press
Charleston, SC
www.historypress.com

Front cover, top and bottom, right: Unidentified early twentieth-century prostitutes. *Courtesy of Jay Moynihan. Top, center:* Evangelist Billy Sunday. *Courtesy of the Library of Congress.*
Back cover, top, center: Prohibition-era bar scene. *Courtesy of the American Prohibition Museum.*

First published 2024

Manufactured in the United States

ISBN 9781467156981

Library of Congress Control Number: 2024938195

CONTENTS

ACKNOWLEDGEMENTS

This book began when as a young professor I started teaching Georgia history at what is today Middle Georgia State University. A native Virginian from the Blue Ridge Mountains, I knew little of the Deep South. But over time and many travels, I came to appreciate the long and colorful history of both Macon and the region. Visits to the Ocmulgee National Monument, the Johnston-Felton-Hay House, Rose Hill Cemetery, the Cannonball House, the Georgia Music Hall of Fame, the Grand Opera House and the Douglass Theatre convinced me that this beautiful city had an abundance of rich stories to tell. But admittedly, I have always been drawn to the darker side of history. And after much research, I found that Macon had a vibrant underworld between 1900 and 1940, one so fascinating that I felt its story needed to be told.

So many people have made this book possible. The staff at the Washington Memorial Library Archives worked tirelessly to help me locate city council minutes and other information that I needed to tell the story I wanted to tell. Without their help, this project would have taken years to complete.

Fortunately, I was able to enlist the help of Jay Moynihan, professor emeritus of criminal justice, with a number of the images I needed for the book. His collection of photographs of prostitutes provided me with some insight into the personality of the ladies who worked the houses in Macon's red-light district.

My sisters Martha Brown and Sherry Cameron have been particularly supportive, always offering encouragement and advice. I am so fortunate to have them by my side.

There are others too, however, who contributed in ways that, perhaps, they never realized. My tennis buddies Chris Wharton, Brooks Fox, and Kelvin Oliver never failed to ask good questions. But importantly, the fun and friendly competition we share on the courts each week gave me a much-needed respite from the hard work of writing and revising.

Although our dear tennis friend John Nichols left us for North Georgia, he provided me with good humor and assistance in my research. His experiences as a young soldier in Middle Georgia gave me a keen look into the underside of Macon during the 1960s.

And there is professor emeritus Beatrice Naff Bailey, known affectionately as Bea to me and my classmates at Franklin County High School, who took time out of her own busy researching and writing schedule to read a couple of chapters and offer advice. She is and always will be my history buddy.

My lead editor, Joe Gartrell, never failed to answer my questions or to offer words of encouragement. His support for this project from beginning to end has been unwavering. Zoe Ames, my copyeditor, read the manuscript thoroughly before it went into production. Her suggestions and revisions significantly improved the narrative.

I would be remiss, however, if I didn't explain just how important my bandmates Donny Screws and Cliff Lee have been to this project. These two incredibly talented musicians have always been supportive of my many endeavors. I am truly blessed to be their brothers in music.

In the end, however, I would have never completed this undertaking without the love and support of my family. My wife, Penny, and our daughter, Rylee, patiently put up with the long hours I spent cloistered in my study researching, writing and revising.

Whatever this book's failings, they are solely my own.

Introduction

OUT OF THE SHADOWS

*E*stablished in 1823 in the heart of some of the South's most productive cotton fields, Macon, Georgia, became one of the state's most wealthy cities by the beginning of the Civil War. Its location on the Ocmulgee River, together with its Central Georgia Railroad, made the city a transportation hub for the cotton trade. Unlike in other southern cities that had developed around this trade, however, Macon's businessmen had invested in railroads, utilities, banking, retail stores and manufacturing. And though the Civil War had a disastrous impact on the state and region, the city, spared the destruction that befell Atlanta, continued to grow. Its diverse economy offered opportunity, and people from New England, the Northeast and the Upper South flocked to the city. By 1900, Macon could boast a population of over forty thousand.[1]

But the city offered its citizens more than just economic opportunity. Macon had a vibrant religious life. Episcopalians, Baptists, Methodists, Presbyterians, Catholics and Jews established churches and synagogues throughout the city. With close to seventy houses of worship on the eve of World War I, its citizens would claim that it was one of the most pious cities in the South.[2]

Macon also prided itself on being a center of higher learning. Mercer Institute, which later became Mercer University in 1871, would offer degrees in the liberal arts, business, law and medicine. Wesleyan College, chartered in 1833, would be the first institution in the nation to offer degrees to women. The Georgia-Alabama Business College, founded in 1889, would

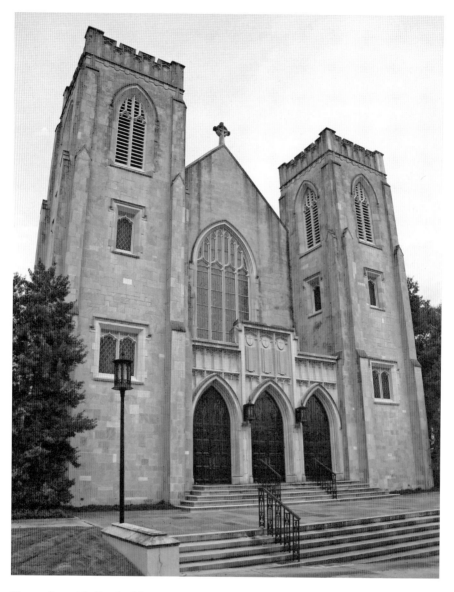

Places of worship like the Mulberry Street Methodist Church, as well as the many other churches in Macon, played a significant role in safeguarding the city's morals. *Courtesy of Mulberry Street Methodist Church.*

provide women as well as men opportunities to become stenographers, secretaries, bookkeepers and accountants. There were preparatory schools like the Georgia Academy for the Blind, established in 1852, and Mount DeSales Academy, which opened in 1876. Unfortunately, during the era of Jim Crow segregation, there were few opportunities for the city's Black citizens to receive an advanced education until the Missionary Baptists founded Central City College, later known as Georgia Baptist College.[3]

The city had a large number of community- and service-oriented clubs and societies. The city directory recorded, in 1905, well over seventy-five organizations such as the Masons, the Elks and the Rotary Club. All were active in raising money for hospitals, orphanages, schools and the indigent.[4]

Macon was unrivaled in the South in terms of its architecture. Situated in the Vineville section and along the tree-lined streets on Coleman Hill overlooking the downtown area were Regency, Georgian, Greek Revival, Italianate, Queen Anne and Victorian houses. Some, like the Johnston-Felton-Hay House, had indoor plumbing, central heat and gas illumination years before most citizens in the nation. Its city hall, auditorium and commercial buildings were also unmatched in terms of their beauty and elegance.

The arts flourished here as well. There were literary and thespian societies, dancing schools and music academies. The city had an opera house. Built in 1884, the Grand, as it was known, had its own orchestra and featured musical and dramatic productions from around the country.

Macon also had one of the most beautiful cemeteries in the country. Rose Hill, founded and designed by Simiri Rose from Connecticut in 1840, had exotic plants and trees gracing its terraced landscape and carriage paths. Here lay the city's most prominent citizens. In later years, it became the last resting place of four of the South's most celebrated musicians: Duane Allman, Berry Oakley, Butch Trucks and Greg Allman.

Macon's citizens had good reason to be proud of their metropolis on the Ocmulgee. But like most prosperous cities, it had a dark side. Since its inception, the city had attracted saloons, gambling houses, dance halls and brothels. Limited in number and removed from the city's center, most operated with little interference from the authorities. Yet at the turn of the twentieth century, the number of such establishments swelled, and many now were open for business in the downtown district and in the more respectable neighborhoods. Macon's reputation as a progressive, sophisticated and cultured religious community was being challenged by a thriving underworld that operated in full view of its residents.

Citizens who walked the streets of Macon in 1905 could find clothing and jewelry stores, flower shops, pharmacies, banks and restaurants. But here were also, according to the 1905 *Macon City Directory*, over sixty saloons, many of them located on Mulberry, Cotton, Poplar, Fourth and

Top: The Johnston-Felton-Hay House, completed in 1859, was not only a preeminent example of Italian Renaissance Revival architecture but also one of the most modern houses in the country in the late nineteenth century. *Courtesy of the Georgia Trust.*

Bottom: Constructed in the 1830s, this Greek Revival mansion on Coleman Hill, known today as the Woodruff House, symbolized for Macon's citizens and visitors the simple elegance of antebellum architecture. *Courtesy of the* New Georgia Encyclopedia.

The Grand Opera House, built in the 1890s, had an orchestra and featured plays and musicals from around the country. This picture was taken in 1905, soon after its interior was remodeled. *Courtesy of the Grand Opera House.*

Fifth Streets, that offered both beer and hard liquor to their patrons. This was an exponential increase from 1880, when the city directory recorded only twenty saloons in Macon.[5]

Legally off limits to women, such establishments were gathering places for local men, be they workmen at the city's mills, railroads and foundries or businessmen, bankers and attorneys who had offices downtown. Some saloons, placed near the more fashionable hotels like the European, the Brown House or the Hotel Lanier, were ornate in design and offered wide selections of liquors and cocktails. Others, situated in alleys and side streets, were known as tippling houses, somewhat spartan in layout and selling only shots of whiskey. Many of these same low-rent establishments had a reputation for selling liquor to young boys and the streetwalkers who plied their trade in the more remote sections of the city.

In the saloons and taverns, men could debate the politics and issues of the day, but they also could discuss the latest baseball or football scores and the results of boxing matches. Here, too, were opportunities to find card games, craps, roulette wheels and tickets for lotteries and numbers rackets in the city.

Macon, by the early 1900s, had become known as a gambler's paradise. Gambling houses and back-alley card and craps games were pervasive. Fortunes were won and lost in only a few minutes in the many poker and faro games that ran throughout the city. And with the introduction of slot machines, many men and young boys saw their earnings disappear with only a few pulls of the handle.

But it was probably the numerous lotteries operating in the city that took the most money out of Macon citizens' pockets. For only a few cents or up to ten dollars, a player could bet on a sequence of numbers that might match the total sales of stocks and bonds for a particular day. If a player hit, there was a considerable payoff. But the chances of winning were 999 to 1.

If one was unlucky at the gaming tables or the numbers rackets, one could possibly find solace with one of the many prostitutes who now resided in the growing number of brothels that made Macon their home. Scattered throughout the city, these houses of ill repute often had elegant and refined interiors, with young women who were well schooled in how to please their patrons. But most bawdy houses in the city were less sophisticated. Many were little more than cribs that offered a lady of the evening and her client a bed for an hour or two.

Just why many women in Macon chose this life is debatable. The city did have mills, shops and offices that could afford them an honest, albeit meager, living. Perhaps this in itself is the answer. The pay a young single woman received for one week's "honest" work was less than what she could make in one evening entertaining a lonely man.

Much to the horror of ministers and reformers, the city now had an underworld no longer operating in the shadows but in the open, with little fear of the authorities. Macon, they believed, was firmly in the grips of a culture of vice, and they demanded that the mayor and city council do something.

They did. Around 1913, all women who ran houses of ill fame were forced to relocate their businesses to a predominantly Black neighborhood below the Central of Georgia Railroad tracks. Known historically as Tybee, the area now became the city's protected red-light district. Although it was "officially" closed in 1917, it continued to remain, for years afterward, a place where prostitutes, gambling houses and blind tigers could operate with only minimal interference from the police.

This, of course, was not what the city's ministers and reformers wanted. It also was not, in the opinion of many health professionals, a solution to the growing problem of venereal disease. And so, from the first years of the twentieth century to the end of World War II, a battle raged in Macon for both the soul and the health of the city.

Chapter 1

NO REST FOR THE WICKED

At the beginning of the twentieth century, ministers, civic organizations and social reformers across the country initiated a Purity Crusade to rid cities of all forms of social evil. Macon was to be no exception. By eliminating alcohol, prurient literature, prostitution and gambling, for example, Macon's reformers believed they could improve, maybe even perfect, the moral and spiritual lives of fallen men and women. They were relentless in their determination to save the city from the sin and immorality that they believed threatened to destroy all that was good and decent in American life. As a consequence, there was to be no respite for those who both enjoyed and profited from Macon's underworld.

Whiskey and saloons had been an integral part of southern culture since the early 1800s. Unlike in New England and the Midwest, during the nineteenth century, men in the South, whether in taverns or at home, drank large quantities of hard liquor every day. Whiskey, the preferred drink, was also consumed at community events, elections and even during the mustering of the militia. Liquor was ever present and was associated with good living and manliness.[6]

But heavy drinking took its toll on not only men but also women and children. Husbands and fathers died or were critically injured in drinking-related accidents and violent confrontations. Many succumbed to liver disease or became so dependent on whiskey that they were unable to work and care for their families. Something had to be done about the South's drinking problem.[7]

Prohibition organizations like the Woman's Christian Temperance Union, however, had never been strong in the South—that is, until the late nineteenth century and early twentieth. It was then that there was something of a Great Awakening in the region. Church attendance increased, and evangelists attracted thousands to their revivals. Men were called on to repent and give up alcohol, gambling, lechery and other vices.[8]

It was during this same time that southern ministers became active in the Anti-Saloon League. Formed in 1893 in Ohio, the league's initial objective was to put pressure on city officials to shut down the places where men customarily drank liquor or beer. But by the early 1900s, it had broadened its mission and demanded that southern politicians support the adoption of prohibition on both the state and national level.[9]

Macon's ministers embraced the cause. Despite its beauty, its churches, its colleges and its bustling businesses and factories, the city, they believed, was in the clutches of liquor dealers and saloonkeepers. The adoption of prohibition in the state would free the city's men and their families from the evils of alcohol.

But it would also go far, they believed, in protecting the virtue of White women. Speaking to a large crowd at the Macon auditorium, Judge W.A. Covington, a leader in the fight for prohibition in the state, said the law would keep liquor out of the hands of "some vicious negro" who might, under its influence, be inclined to assault a White woman. The women of Georgia "who always stood in dread of drunken negroes," declared the judge, would now be safer.[10]

After the 1906 race riot in Atlanta, many came to share Judge Covington's view and supported prohibition in the belief that it would help contain the violent and lascivious tendencies of Black men. The riot or massacre stemmed from unsubstantiated reports in the *Atlanta Constitution* and the *Atlanta Journal* of Black men assaulting White women in the city. A mob of White men formed in the downtown area on September 24 and began attacking any Black person or Black business they came upon. The violence continued into the following day. Finally, the mob was dispersed, but not before over twenty-five Blacks and two Whites were killed.[11]

The blame, many believed, was traceable to liquor and the saloons that Blacks frequented in the city. As with the implementation of disfranchisement, it was argued that prohibition would assist Whites in their efforts to keep Blacks in their place. Legislators agreed and passed both statewide prohibition and a series of laws restricting Black voting.

As a result, on December 31, 1907, Georgia became the first state in the South to adopt prohibition. At the insistence of prohibition advocates, the law was quite draconian. It not only made the manufacture and sale of alcohol illegal but also banned the keeping and giving away of intoxicants in public places.[12]

Macon's ministers and the Anti-Saloon League rejoiced. Meeting in Atlanta in November 1907, the league explained how the new law, if enforced properly, was going to impact the lives of Georgians: "We honestly believe that the enforcement of the prohibition law will contribute largely to the material prosperity, to the intellectual development, to the moral improvement, to the domestic happiness and to the spiritual growth of the people of our state." Prohibition, they assured citizens, would change Macon and other Georgia cities for the better.[13]

It wasn't long before Macon's ministers, the Anti-Saloon League and city officials realized that enforcement would prove to be a challenge. Even though the state's prohibition law was very restrictive, there were loopholes. Georgia, for example, allowed the members of fraternal orders and civic clubs to keep liquor in so-called lockers. Each organization, however, had to pay a $500 fee for the privilege. It was not long before resourceful men in the city began forming "locker clubs" for the sole purpose of keeping and drinking liquor.

The state also allowed cities to license saloons to sell near beer, a fermented malt beverage that contained less than 1 percent alcohol. Saloonkeepers quickly discovered that this presented them with an opportunity to also sell whiskey, albeit discreetly. Soon, well over fifty saloons were operating throughout the city—all, with only a few exceptions, selling hard liquor and wine.

The city's police department frequently raided saloons that they knew were selling liquor. Many of these raids were successful and turned up large caches of whiskey hidden in secret rooms. Acting on the testimony of several draymen who had been delivering whiskey to saloons in the city, the county sheriff and the police department commandeered a large "auto dray," as trucks were then called, and began a series of raids on the evening of May 10, 1911. The operation led to the confiscation of forty barrels of whiskey and eighteen cases of liquor of varying brands. But despite indictments and heavy fines, the liquor kept flowing in the ever-growing number of saloons in the city.[14]

By 1913, the mayor, city council and concerned citizens had decided that the situation was out of control. At the urging of the Anti-Saloon League and the League for Law and Order, they agreed to deny saloon licenses to less-than-reputable businessmen and adopt restrictions that would assist law enforcement in spotting saloonkeepers who were selling whiskey. All establishments, for example, would be required to label beverage containers with their contents and the manufacturer's name. In addition, no saloon would be allowed to have frosted windows, screens, curtains or any other obstruction that would prevent law officers from surveilling the goings-on inside an establishment. And believing that Blacks were more inclined to violence and lawlessness after drinking whiskey, the council decided to limit the number of saloons that would be allowed in predominantly Black communities like Tybee.[15]

In the same year, Macon appointed a new police chief who pledged to "wipe out whiskey in Macon's saloons." Beginning in December, Chief George S. Riley Sr., together with a squad of six plainclothes officers, began a series of raids in the downtown district. As a result, the chief and his men were able to seize "enough whiskey to float a battleship." But the raids had minimal impact. The chief was only able to net four saloonkeepers. This was insignificant in a city with over fifty saloons, all or most in violation of the law.[16]

The locker clubs were, in the opinion of the city councilmen, an even greater problem. Since the prohibition law had been adopted, the council had been flooded with applications by ad hoc organizations to allow their members to store whiskey in their personal lockers or cabinets. Soon "phony" locker clubs, as councilmen described them, could be found throughout the city, operating not as clubs but as barrooms for profit. "Seventy-five percent of the locker clubs," said Alderman W.H. Fetner in a council meeting in April 1911, "are blind tigers, running wide open." More whiskey, he concluded, was available in Macon than ever before.[17]

The locker clubs were abhorrent to Macon's citizens and officials in other ways. It was not uncommon, for example, for club members to drink and celebrate on Sundays, a vile offense to a city that prided itself on its large churchgoing population. But worse, they violated the laws and social codes of Jim Crow segregation. "It is simply disgusting the way these clubs are now run," declared Alderman Steve Wright in the April meeting. "They are nothing but open saloons, and there ought to be some way to restrict them. I am told that negroes visit these white locker clubs and make purchases of liquor and beer, whether for themselves or others, I don't know. That should not be allowed."[18]

The debate over how best to deal with the "phony" locker clubs continued for several years. But after investigating the legalities, the city council concluded in late 1914 that it had the authority to close all clubs that were not fraternal orders with national charters. Beginning in 1915, only the Elks, the Eagles and the Owls clubs would be permitted to store liquor in their clubhouses.[19]

While the leaders of the Anti-Saloon League and the League for Law and Order welcomed the closure of the bogus drinking clubs, they believed that the raids and the new restrictions on saloons were doing little to curtail violations of the law. Since 1913, the two organizations had employed detectives to visit every saloon in the city. In every case but one, they were able to purchase liquor. With this evidence and the assistance of attorney R.D. Feagin, the law enforcement branch of the Anti-Saloon League filed thirty-four petitions for injunctions against the establishments.[20]

Dr. W.N. Ainsworth, pastor of Mulberry Street Methodist Church, one of the key spokesmen for the city's League for Law and Order, put saloonkeepers on notice. The league, he claimed, had ample financial resources and would "persist in its prosecution until every saloon is put out of business through the aid of the courts by the injunction process." Dr. Ainsworth maintained that he and the members of the league had no animosity toward the saloonkeepers, but "the law is going to be vindicated and society protected, if it takes a few jails and enlarged road gangs to hold the determined outlaws." But Dr. Ainsworth did offer saloonkeepers a proposition. If they would surrender their licenses and pledge to quit the business forever, the league would drop its injunctions against them.[21]

BISHOP W. N. AINSWORTH

Dr. W.N. Ainsworth, who served as president of Wesleyan College and as pastor of Mulberry Street Methodist Church, was a vocal critic of Macon's mayor and city council for tolerating saloons and a vice district. He crusaded until his death in 1942 for the prohibition of alcohol in the state and nation. *Courtesy of the Macon* Telegraph.

The proprietors, however, were not ready to throw in the towel. The liquor trade was extremely profitable and well worth the risks, in their minds. Determined to keep their businesses open, saloonkeepers and their attorneys used every legal tactic they could muster to delay and obstruct the effort to shut them down.

But the league was relentless. Finally, after exhausting every recourse, the saloonkeepers agreed to come to terms. In February 1916, over fifty saloonkeepers gathered in the recorder's court to sign affidavits stating that they would never again engage in the sale of liquor, wine or beer within Macon and the Bibb County limits as long as the trade was illegal. They then surrendered their national, state and city licenses and agreed to cooperate with city officials and law enforcement in suppressing violations of the city and state prohibition laws. If the men failed to live up to the agreement, they would be prosecuted. "For First Time In History," read a headline in the *Macon News* on February 26, "Macon Will Be Without Even 'Near Beer' Saloons of Any Kind."[22]

The end of licensed near beer saloons in the city, however, did not stop the liquor trade or the operation of speakeasies and blind tigers. So named for disguising their businesses as exhibitions of exotic animals, these illegal bars gave their customers a shot of whiskey for the price of admission. Macon had a blind tiger ordinance, but these establishments were difficult to locate. They were often hidden in concealed rooms or apartments and scattered throughout the city, and law enforcement rarely succeeded in breaking up their operations. When they did make arrests, they discovered that the city ordinance was too vague to bring formal charges against the accused.

But in February 1916, the liquor-related killing of a young girl in downtown Macon spurred the League for Law and Order and church congregations to action. On the evening of February 14, Rosa Lee Eubanks, twenty, was walking to her home to prepare for a Valentine's social at Centenary Methodist Church when she was suddenly hit by a bullet fired from a speeding taxi. The bullet pierced her heart, and she died in the arms of a patrolman who was near the scene.[23]

The shooter, D.B. "Doc" Branam, was soon arrested and charged. Branam's nephew, who was with him in the car, stated that his uncle was on a drunken spree and that he was firing his pistol at random. Although no one other than Rosa was injured or killed, one of Branam's bullets did smash the window of Dr. J.P. Holmes's vehicle. Fortunately, no one was in the car with Dr. Holmes.[24]

Dr. Ainsworth was so enraged by the killing that he blamed the mayor and city council for Rosa's death. According to the pastor, the blind tiger from which Branam got his liquor had been operating in an alley with the full knowledge of city authorities. They, in his opinion, were far worse than the man who killed her. The "blood of Miss Rosa Lee Eubanks," he declared, "is upon the hands of the authorities who licensed this place, and continue to let it run there in defiance of decency and law."[25]

Dr. Ainsworth's accusations did not go unanswered. The mayor and council said he had no evidence that city officials had not been doing their utmost to bring lawbreakers to justice and that his attacks were nothing less than slander. "If this man realized the fact that we knew it was going on and that we protected it, why has he not raised a kick," asked the council. Indignant, the councilmen further stated that "the man who shot down that innocent girl in cold blood is bad enough, but the man who will attempt to rape the character of his fellow man is far worse."[26]

The pastor did not back down. City officials, he believed, had not only been lax in enforcing the law but also, perhaps, complicit in allowing blind tigers to operate without interference. "These saloons are a menace to everything our people hold dear. They have been tolerated in defiance of the law long enough. The people have spoken. The death of Rosa Lee Eubanks must be avenged. The liquor business in Macon must go."[27]

And so, at the behest of the Law and Order League, the city council instructed the police department to shut down as many blind tigers as possible. But as before, the effort met with little success. The traffic in liquor would continue unabated, for the most part, in Macon throughout the prohibition era.

EVEN IF THE TRADE in liquor had been stopped, other destructive vices, said reformers, flourished in the city. Situated along alleys, down backstreets and on the main throughfares of the downtown area, for example, were gambling houses where sporting gentlemen could bet on horse races and baseball, try their luck at craps and the roulette wheel or play card games like poker and faro. The men who ran these houses were also bookmakers and profited handsomely from lotteries and the numbers racket.

For the most part, gamblers were left alone. But as the number of gambling houses proliferated, ministers came to believe that the city was becoming known as a haven for moral depravity. As in their crusade against whiskey and blind tigers, they would threaten and cajole Macon's city officials into adopting and enforcing new laws against gambling.

Beginning in 1903, Dr. J.L. White of the First Baptist Church organized a campaign "to stand for men and measures" that would "secure passage of ordinances that would secure an honest and pure administration of the city." To achieve this, Dr. White called for the creation of a Law and Order League composed of members of all churches.[28]

But before they could go after the gambling houses, ministers claimed, church members must first start with themselves. In a sermon delivered at the Mulberry Street Methodist Church in January 1904, Dr. W.N. Ainsworth denounced the playing of cards as a form of idleness that "was a wide-spread curse of human society, and a violation of the order of God." The card table, said the pastor, led to gambling, a disease that was permeating every sector and home in society. Even playing cards as a family diversion was dangerous. "I would no more play cards with my children than I would play with rattle snakes." Boys who become experts at cards, he stated, turn to gambling. And once hooked, they would later wreck the homes of their families. "I know the social card table holds a vital connection with the gambling of the age," he concluded.[29]

This was the message of many of the evangelists who came to Macon. During two weeks of services held at the city auditorium, the Grand Opera House and even the foundries, machine works and railroad shops in March 1905, Reverend George Stuart called attention to the card-playing "fashionable social clubs" that infested Macon. It was in such clubs that society women, unbeknownst to the public, were playing bridge and other games for prizes. Whether for money or a fancy vase, gambling, he said, was gambling and a sin before God.[30]

Later, in April, the fiery Methodist evangelist Sam Jones also attacked society women who spent more time playing cards and drinking wine and spiked punch in their clubs than at church or at home. "A woman has got no more business in a club than she has in hell," he declared. "How in the name of God can a woman properly fulfill her duties as a mother or a wife," he asked, "when instead of being at home with her husband or her children, she is off at some club tanked up on wine or beer?" The behavior of these society women at their clubs was not only disgraceful but also evil. "To my mind the most diabolical sight these days is to see a lot of women leaning over a punch bowl at some fashionable club like a lot of suckling pigs around a trough."[31]

Dr. J.L. White echoed these sentiments a month later and called on the members of his congregation to avoid social clubs and rid their homes of the gambler's tools. "Let us have a number of bonfires in the homes of Macon tonight. Burn all the cards that you can get your hands on, for don't you know they are the identical same cards that the gambler uses on his table." He wasn't sure whether law enforcement would ever be able to do away with gambling in the city, but he did believe that "the law of God can break up gambling in your own life." It was time to "stop it now and turn to God."[32]

There was hope for Macon. In the same sermon, Dr. White commended the police department for recent raids on gambling houses and the fact that it was now confiscating all gaming paraphernalia. But raids, he said, should continue nonstop. "Raid them every night and every hour....An occasional

Left: Sam Jones, the fiery evangelist who conducted revivals in Macon and other southern cities in the early 1900s, denounced not only liquor but also society women who played cards and drank spiked punch. *Courtesy of Rose Lawn Museum.*

Below: Before the construction of the present building in 1925, this wooden structure served as Macon's auditorium. Here, itinerant evangelists and Macon's ministers held revivals and rallies to denounce liquor, dancing, card playing and prostitution. *Courtesy of Middle Georgia Archives, Washington Memorial Library.*

raid will not break up the practice, but a continuance of the good work, recently started, will doubtless break it up."[33]

The numerous sermons, editorials and petitions demanding a vigorous campaign against all gambling in the city were having an effect. The city council, now under pressure to cleanse Macon of all gambling, decided to go after the gambling houses. In 1911, the new Bibb County sheriff stated that he would not rest until he had rid the city of the gaming tables, the lotteries and the numbers racket. Macon, many thought, was well on its way to becoming a city free of vice.

CONTRIBUTING TO THE VICE that ministers and reformers saw all around them during the early 1900s were the new fashions that were taking hold in Macon. One thing they found alarming was the growing popularity of jazz dancing. Whether at college functions, private parties or some of the newly opened dance clubs like the Sunken Garden, located beneath the Bibb National Bank building on the corner of Cherry and Second Street, young people were enjoying the syncopated rhythms of ragtime and a new kind of music that was coming to be known as jazz.

Born in New Orleans before World War I, this new improvisational music encouraged various forms of dancing that many found too sensual and vulgar. Some ministers and city officials expressed their alarm at what they believed to be "nothing more than a prolonged sex orgy set to music."[34] Some even thought that the new dances encouraged attitudes and behavior that could lead to violence. Dr. W.N. Ainsworth said, for example, that if fathers and husbands saw performed in their parlors what was taking place in the ballrooms of Macon, someone would get shot.

Despite these concerns, young people kept dancing, with little backlash from society's guardians of morality. But in the years immediately following World War I, there emerged a number of new steps that alarmed even professional teachers of dance. Meeting in New York in 1919, the American National Association of the Masters of Dancing said new jazz dances such as the wriggle, the crawl, the dip, the bend and the shimmy were ruining all that was elegant and refined in the art. The most offensive, the members agreed, was the shimmy. This new dance was performed at varying rhythms and tempos, with dancers gyrating their shoulders and hips in a way that conservative onlookers found overly exuberant and sexually suggestive. Just who originated the dance is unclear, but one thing was certain: it had to go. Miss Birdie Blackshear, a Macon dance instructor

Ministers and dance teachers in Macon thought the "shimmy" was vulgar and sexually provocative. They called on the mayor and city council to ban the dance in public places. *Public domain.*

who attended the meeting, said she was "positive the association would wipe the shimmy off the map."[35]

Earlier in 1919, Miss Blackshear had invited a committee of ministers, the mayor, the city council and representatives from social clubs to a demonstration of the dances that were now in vogue in the city. Most of the modern dances, she said, were artistic when properly done, but the city's uninstructed young people were corrupting them with sensual contortions. She charged that "the shimmy-wabble, the cheek-to-cheek, and the tickle-toe are vulgar and are being 'butchered' in Macon."[36] And based on her observations, the dances as performed by the city's youth were "unsanitary, as the faces of the dancers are pressed together and assists in the spread of disease." She believed that the dances should be barred by city ordinance.[37]

Even before attending the demonstration, Macon's ministers were decrying such dances and asking that they be prohibited by law. Dr. G.H. Fern, pastor of First Christian Church and president of the Macon Ministerial Union, said he believed Christians should practice "total

English-born evangelist Gypsy Smith, shown here in his Salvation Army uniform, held revivals in the Macon city auditorium during the years before World War I. He vehemently denounced dancing, believing that most women who turned to prostitution got their start in the dance halls. *Courtesy of the Library of Congress.*

abstinence" from dancing since, in his opinion, it was nothing more than "hugging to music." He advocated a "national-wide prohibition of all dancing," but doubting such a measure would ever be adopted, he believed all Christians should join the movement "to do away with the cheek-to-cheek, tickle-toe, and the shimmy-wabble."[38]

This had been the message of many of the evangelists who came to town. Speaking before a large audience in the city auditorium in 1916, Gypsy Smith denounced all dancing as of the devil. Dancing, said Smith, was nothing more than a "sexual love feast" that had "led to the downfall of 350,000 of the 500,000 impure girls in America today." It was, he proclaimed, the "training ship for hell."[39]

Like Smith, Macon's ministers warned their congregations about the danger dancing posed for young women. Taking as his subject "Jesus Christ or the Modern Dance," Reverend W.L. Hamrick of Mabel White Baptist Church, for example, said that modern dances should be "driven from society." Doing so, he said, would save young women from falling into debauchery, as it was his belief that a majority of the country's fallen women could trace their history to the dance halls. Near the end of his sermon, he rolled up his sleeves and declared that he was prepared to clean up the town himself if necessary. He then challenged Macon's citizens to join him in ridding the city of all decadence.[40]

Already, there were those in the city who prohibited dances that they thought were vulgar in their ballrooms and resorts. Frank Hodges, the manager of Lakeside Pavilion, posted rules on the facility's walls regulating the kinds of dances its patrons were allowed to perform. Hodges asked policemen to assist him in removing couples who did the shimmy-wabble from the dance floor.

After witnessing variations of jazz dancing, all those present at Miss Blackshear's studio concluded that they were indeed vulgar. The committee of ministers all agreed that they would urge members of their congregations to stop their sons and daughters from engaging in what they believed was not only inappropriate but also sinful behavior.

Members of the council, including the mayor, pledged to take action in the form of an ordinance that would ban sexually suggestive dancing from public places. If it was adopted, Macon would not be an outlier. Atlanta, Savannah, Americus and other Georgia cities had passed similar ordinances by 1920, as had Philadelphia, New York, Chicago and Cleveland. But how was the ordinance to be enforced? Would police officers now be patrolling clubs, ballrooms and college functions in search of unsuspecting dancers who dared flout the law? Evidently, city officials hoped the uproar over dances like the shimmy would fade away. A search of the city council minutes, the city code and newspapers indicates that no anti-shimmy law was ever passed.[41]

But the opposition to dancing in all its forms continued on into 1920. In that same year, ministers learned that the National Association of Dancing Masters had named a new dance after John Wesley, the founder of Methodism. The "Wesleyan Slow Step," said ministers, was an insult to all denominations and an abomination before God. Reverend T.F. Callaway of the Tabernacle Baptist Church wondered what would come next: "An Episcopal Hug, a Presbyterian Jazz, a Christian Hop, a John the Baptist Jumper"?[42]

Reverend Callaway went so far as to attack all modern dancing as destructive of morality. In his "Fifty Reasons Why Dancing Is Wrong," he explained point by point just how the gyrations and the hugging that most dances promoted led to the debasement of young people. Young women were particularly vulnerable. "Many a mother's daughter does not realize that she is being led captive over the smooth-waxed floor, by some fierce, lustful, gloat-eyed brute."

Most dances, he argued, came from inferior races and decadent cities. The names given modern dances were evidence enough of "their bestiality and heathenism."

"The Tango" from the natives of South America, which is worse than the "Hooche-Kooche." "The Grizzly Bear" gets its name from the bear-like hug assumed by the dancers and originated with the negroes in San Francisco. The "Turkey Trot" was first seen on the Bowery in New York, and it is well known that the old, slow, round waltz found its origin in the low places of Paris. And we might assume that the "Fox Trot," the "Buzzard Jazz," the "El Gato" (or Gate to Hell) or even the "Wesleyan" will not be an improvement on their predecessors.[43]

Callaway claimed that even the Dancing Masters themselves agreed with his assessment. "Dancing today is the most degrading thing on earth," said the organization at its twenty-third annual meeting in Boston in 1920. "It is demoralizing our young people. If it is allowed to go on it will bring the country to ruin. It is indecent and disgusting."[44]

MODERN DANCING AND THE dance halls, along with alcohol and other vices, many believed, were responsible for the growing number of prostitutes who openly plied their trade on the streets and in the numerous brothels that could be found throughout Macon. The city's ministers and reformers admitted that some of these women fully embraced their profession but that there were many others who had been seduced by unscrupulous men and women into surrendering their virginity and turning to prostitution. This "White slave trade," they argued, pervaded the country and was alive and well in Macon.

There was evidence that young women were falling prey to prostitution rings in the country's cities. Ernest A. Bell, a Methodist missionary who was active in the anti-vice campaign in Chicago, recounted his struggles against forced prostitution in his book *Fighting the Traffic in Young Girls* (1910). Clifford Roe, a crusading Chicago prosecutor who made the fight his life's work, documented actual cases of White slavery in such books as *Panders and Their White Slaves* (1910), *Horrors of the White Slave Trade* (1911) and *The Girl Who Disappeared* (1914). Both men's exposés on the dark underworld of prostitution alarmed the public and put pressure on congress to pass the Mann Act in 1910, which made it a federal crime to transport a woman across state lines for illicit purposes.[45]

Before Bell and Roe published their findings, organizations and missions had already been founded in cities around the country to redeem "fallen women." With the help of Charles N. Crittenton, a New York millionaire turned evangelist, one such mission, the Door of Hope, was established in Macon in 1900. Crittenton, who visited Macon seeking support for the mission's work in 1901, explained he had discovered that "fallen women" did not come from any particular class. In fact, he had encountered many who were well educated and from respectable homes. However, they all tended to have one thing in common: they had been deceived by a charming but lascivious man.[46]

A.W. Elliot, who established the Southern Rescue Mission for young girls, had reached the same conclusion. According to Elliot, those responsible for the degradation of young women were "worthless men in the South who do practically no work and wear the very finest clothing...and...their daily and nightly vocation is gambling." These vipers, he maintained, were always lying in wait for innocent girls that they could lure into moral degeneracy.[47]

Elliot, like others who investigated White slavery, asserted that young single women were at their most vulnerable in city rail stations. In response, the Traveler's Aid Society was created. Its purpose, said its founders, was to prevent unsuspecting young women from being misled into prostitution.

> *Agents of disorderly houses travel on trains to secure victims. Every year thousands of young women come to the cities, looking for honorable livelihood. Many fall easy prey to the unscrupulous persons always lying in wait for travelers, who use every means to take advantage of the unfriended, the ignorant, the timid stranger.*[48]

By posting warning signs and stationing its guardians at rail stations in Macon and other cities, the society believed it could save young women from predators. The police committee of the Macon city council applauded their work and decided in 1915 that it would deputize a special squad of matrons to patrol the city's rail stations.[49]

To ensure that young women were not being held against their will in the city's brothels, a special White slave agent was appointed in 1912. C.A. Cunningham, acting under the authority of the city council, inspected any and all houses that might be involved in the White slave trade. As per city orders, Cunningham was required to ask all proprietresses of suspected houses of ill fame to fill out information cards on all new girls they had taken in.[50]

But as early as 1913, there was growing doubt that much could be done to save women from prostitution. Some, like Elliot, had come to believe that all "fallen women" had chosen the profession of their own volition. In *The Cause of the Social Evil and Its Remedy* (1914), he disavowed his previous assertions that most prostitutes had been unknowingly lured into the profession. After years of trying to rescue prostitutes, he had realized that most had no interest in reforming and that those who entered the profession did so willingly, not under duress. There was nothing rescue work could do to end the social evil. The only possible solution lay not with legislation or collective action but with families and the individual.[51]

Elliot also had a warning for cities like Atlanta that sought to close their red-light districts. Based on his experience, he said, this would only lead to brothels and prostitutes scattering throughout the city. The best way to aid these women, and society, was to segregate them into a restricted district where they could be regulated.[52]

Nevertheless, there were ministers and reformers in Macon who wanted all brothels closed. But shuttering them, thought city officials, was a near impossibility. According to the city code, closing a suspected brothel would require direct evidence, presented to the mayor and council, that it was operating as a "house of ill-fame." If the city council agreed that the evidence was sufficient, the occupants of the house would then be given five days to leave the city.[53] This was complicated by the fact that a majority of madams rented their houses. Closing them would take money out of the pockets of their landlords, many of whom were some of the city's most prominent businessmen. Macon's merchants would also be impacted. Madams and prostitutes shopped at the city's grocers, clothing stores and furniture dealers. Fearing a backlash from merchants and landlords, the council was reluctant to close establishments that had been deemed "houses of ill-fame."

The best approach, the councilmen believed, was to move all brothels to an area beyond the business district and respectable neighborhoods. Although this was not recorded in the official minutes, sometime between 1905 and 1910, the city council decided that all houses of ill fame would have to relocate to the section of the city below Fifth Street known as the Tybee District. There the houses could operate without police interference as long as they caused no public disturbance. Macon, like Atlanta, New Orleans, Memphis and a number of other southern cities, would now have a protected red-light district.[54]

Chapter 2

A BABYLON BEYOND THE TRACKS

When the city council decided to move all brothels to the Tybee section of the city, they believed that few people would object. Tybee was poor, Black and some distance from the business district and the respectable neighborhoods. For a number of years, the relocation of the houses went unnoticed. But by 1915, this section of the city had developed an infamous reptation. In Tybee, known as the city's official red-light district, Whites and Blacks lived cheek by jowl and operated brothels, gambling houses, juke joints and blind tigers, with little police interference.[55]

Tybee came by its name during the founding of Macon, when settlers labored to clear land and drain swamps to make the new city habitable. The work was hard, and the threat of malaria and yellow fever loomed. Slaves less susceptible to these diseases, they thought, such as those who worked the rice and cotton plantations on the barrier island of Tybee, would be needed to complete the task. Another predominantly Black section of the city, Yamacraw Bluff, the original site of the city of Savannah, got its name for similar reasons.

With the end of slavery and the implementation of Jim Crow segregation, many of the city's poorer Black residents settled in Tybee and created a community and a culture all their own. By the early 1900s, it had two grammar schools, one on Hazel Street and another on Turpin. There were a number of churches: Macedonia Baptist, Thankful Baptist, Friendship Baptist and Baptist Tabernacle. There was also a mission for wayward boys and girls located on Hazel Street.[56]

Top: Young women, who labored for long hours with minimal pay in Macon's cotton mills and other factories, often found they could make more money entertaining men at one of the many brothels that operated in the Tybee District. *Courtesy of the Library of Congress.*

Bottom: Macon cotton mill workers pose for a picture inside their place of work. *Courtesy of the Library of Congress.*

While there are no records of Black-owned businesses in the community at the beginning of the twentieth century, there were quite a few industries located either in or close to Tybee that provided employment opportunities. At the Southern Phosphate Company, Mallary and Taylor Iron Works, Massie and Felton Lumber Yard, Buckeye Cotton Oil Company, Acme Brewing Company and the Central Georgia Railroad, for example, men worked in varying capacities, as porters, crosstie cutters, draymen and brakemen. Others found jobs in the city's business district as janitors, waiters, bartenders and cabdrivers.

Women in Tybee had fewer opportunities available to them. According to the 1905 city directory, most worked as laundresses, cooks, maids and seamstresses. Given the large number of single and widowed women who were, according to the directory, unemployed, it's quite possible that many of them worked as prostitutes.[57]

This would not be surprising. Even before Tybee became the city's protected red-light district, it was known to have an underworld of sporting men and women who enjoyed every known vice. Card and craps games, pool halls, blind tigers, streetwalkers and brothels could be found throughout the district.

ALTHOUGH TYBEE WAS HISTORICALLY a Black community, it became integrated by 1915, with White women making up a large share of its residents. A search of Macon's city directory for that year reveals that there were well over one hundred single White women and girls living in the district. Since their occupations weren't listed, it's reasonable to assume that most were prostitutes. There were many other White women in Tybee who were recorded in the directory as being married, although no husband was indicated. This was not unusual. Madams invariably took the title Mrs. and listed their occupation as proprietress of a boardinghouse.[58]

The women who lived and worked in the houses in Tybee were not unlike those in other red-light districts. Many had come from the countryside or small towns near Macon to work in the mills and had grown dispirited with the low wages and long hours and turned to prostitution. There were others who had at one time or another worked the streets and brothels of Atlanta and other cities but grew tired of both the competition and the police harassment. Macon's notoriety as a bustling, wealthy town with a protected vice district made it an attractive place to ply their trade.

But unlike the red-light districts of New York, Chicago, New Orleans and Atlanta, Tybee had only a few fine homes with modern conveniences. Most prostitutes lived and worked in modest houses with no indoor plumbing or electricity. The madams who oversaw the business end of the profession, for the most part, did not own their houses. Instead, out of financial necessity and the need, at times, to easily move to a different location, they rented property from many of the city's prominent businessmen who lived outside the district. These landlords profited handsomely from the trade in Tybee, often getting double the rent that they received for houses in the more respectable neighborhoods.

Many others in the city benefitted financially from the district. Madams and prostitutes, for example, purchased clothing, groceries and home furnishings on a regular basis from merchants in the downtown area.

While most of the houses of prostitution in Tybee were plain and unadorned, some were relatively spacious and well appointed. *Courtesy of Jay Moynihan.*

Not surprisingly, bootleggers did a steady business keeping the houses well supplied with liquor, beer and wine. And while there is no hard evidence of graft, it's quite possible the city's law officers and politicians received kickbacks from madams and landlords in exchange for keeping the district open.

Tybee's thriving business in prostitution was attributable in part to its location. As it was situated near the city terminal station on Fifth Street, customers had only a short walk to any one of its brothels. Business was also spurred by the use of advertising. As in other cities, information books and pamphlets detailing locations, services offered and the price of an evening's assignation were available in terminals from young men and boys who worked as agents for the houses.

Tybee's proximity to the city's railyards, cotton mills, foundries and fertilizer plants was also especially advantageous. At the end of their day or night shifts, many laborers took time to visit their favorite brothels and prostitutes in the district. But the busiest time was right after payday, when industrial workers, temporarily flush with money, provided the houses with a regular stream of customers.

The Macon Terminal, situated near the Tybee District, provided prostitutes and their agents with opportunities to arrange sexual encounters with newcomers to the city. *Courtesy of Exploring Macon.*

Besides sex with the girl of their choice, there were other forms of entertainment available to customers. A number of houses had two or three musicians who supplied dancing music. Some had gaming tables and roulette wheels. Many also served liquor and food. The more upscale houses even offered customers a hot bath with an attentive mistress for the evening.

When the city council unofficially designated Tybee as the city's restricted district, it adopted, as needed, ordinances to regulate prostitutes and the brothels where they lived and worked. Most were designed to make sure that all sex workers remained within the confines of the district and that they not congregate around any neighborhood stores, churches and schools. Nevertheless, they could visit areas beyond Tybee during the day to shop for necessities.[59]

Interestingly, the city sought to restrict a prostitute's mode of transportation if she dared venture beyond Tybee. According to section 696 of the city code, "No woman of ill fame who lived in a bawdy house could ride a horse or bicycle, either in the day time or night, on the streets, or public parks of the city, excepting on the streets below and including Fifth Street." Perhaps this not only kept prostitutes out of the public eye but also limited their ability to solicit clients.[60]

The city council, however, found it difficult to keep prostitutes and brothels from the view of the city's respectable citizens. Despite the order that no "disorderly houses" would be allowed above Fifth Street, madams still attempted to do business in areas outside the district. Between 1910 and 1915, there were numerous accounts in the city newspapers of houses being closed on Pine, Ash, Plum, Second and Broadway. Police Chief George Riley made it clear in January 1914, for example, that "disorderly houses in any respectable section of the city will not be tolerated." The chief, with instructions from the city council, appointed special officers to watch any and all suspicious houses located above Fifth Street. "Since a section has already been designated for disorderly characters," said the chief, he planned "to confine them there or else arraign them before the recorder for punishment."[61]

Keeping order and preventing prostitutes from venturing beyond the restricted district often proved challenging for the four police officers assigned to patrol Tybee day and night. Before 1915, most of the district's prostitutes could come and go as they pleased, many of them regularly attending shows at the Grand Opera House. But after complaints from theatergoers and a number of altercations, they were banned from leaving the district in the evenings. To enforce this, the police placed a curfew bell inside the district. Every night at eight o'clock, an officer rang the bell, signaling that all women were to return to their houses. Any women found outside their houses after the curfew were arrested.[62]

Lawlessness inside the district was often a problem. With legal saloons, blind tigers, back-alley tippling houses and brothels all selling liquor, there was always the possibility of drunken scuffles, stabbings and shootings. Much of this violence was perpetrated by young White men who came to the district at all hours seeking female company, liquor and perhaps a run at the gaming tables.[63]

For example, on November 4, 1910, after an evening of drinking, F.M. Bass and A.D. Green decided to take possession of the district. Wielding pistols, they threatened to shoot the Black occupants of a number of houses if they did not immediately leave. It was then that they entered the homes and destroyed anything and everything they saw. Before being arrested, they succeeded in frightening over half of the Black residents out of the district.[64]

In some cases, intoxicated customers threatened and even brutalized prostitutes. Such incidents seemed to happen more often on Saturday nights, when young men were ready for a good time at the end of their work week. In April 1912, A.H. Henderson, a young man visiting Macon from South Georgia, for example, got drunk and ventured into Mollie Burgamy's brothel on Fifth Street. Dissatisfied with the service he received, he drew a pistol and

In the years before World War I, Mayor Bridges Smith and the city council ordered Police Chief George Riley to station four officers in Tybee to not only maintain order but also make sure its prostitutes stayed within the district. In this 1914 picture of Macon's police department, Mayor Bridges Smith can be seen on the far left. Chief Riley is standing in the center. *Courtesy of Middle Georgia Archives, Washington Memorial Library.*

began firing into the ceiling. Fortunately, neither Mollie nor the ladies in her employ, were injured. A similar incident occurred later in October, when two drunken men, L.S. McClendon and Henry Watts, gained entrance to an unnamed brothel in the district and began firing their pistols. Police quickly responded and arrested the men for discharging weapons in the city and disorderly conduct. Once again, no one was injured.[65]

This was not the case, however, at May Livingston's house the following month. On the evening of November 23, Ira T. Jennings, F.E. Woodward and several other men attempted to gain admittance to her establishment. Seeing that they were drunk, May turned them away. But Jennings and his crew were not to be denied and forced the door open. With the assistance of male friends who were already in the house, May and her girls fought off Jennings and his crew, using beer bottles, fists and guns. May, wielding a shotgun, cornered Jennings and threatened to shoot him if he moved. Jennings tried to overwhelm her, but someone struck him over the head with a beer bottle, leaving him bloodied and dazed.[66]

When police officers arrived, they found the house in complete disarray. Women were still screaming, and Jennings was stumbling about with five severe scalp wounds. On the floor was a young woman by the name of Mae Orthanious; she had been struck in the face with either a pistol or brass knuckles. While no one was seriously injured, Jennings and Woodward were arrested and charged with forcible entry and disorderly conduct.[67]

Some of the men who visited the district became well known to the police. After an evening of heavy drinking, Joe Thompson beat and threatened to kill Louise Carmichael. Fearing for her life, Louise quickly had Thompson, who lived in Houston County, arrested and jailed. A week later, he was out of jail and back in the district causing trouble. This time, he was charged with pulling a knife on Pearl Blankenship. In April, he returned to jail for stripping Lucille Smith of her clothing and flogging her. Such was the price of life in Tybee.[68]

Chapter 3

BY PERSONS UNKNOWN

The members of Macon's demimonde enjoyed the protection of the mayor and council as long as they confined their trade to the Tybee District. But that protection had its limits.

Convinced that Blacks were becoming too assertive, Whites in Georgia, both during and after World War I, frequently resorted to violence as a way of reminding them of their proper place in southern society. As a consequence, Macon's Black citizens, particularly those who lived in Tybee, often found themselves the target of racial violence and intimidation. City officials attempted to bring those responsible to justice, but their efforts were in vain. Macon's White citizens, including some officers of the law, refused to cooperate, choosing to remain silent about the perpetrators' identities.

Racial terror became one of the grim realities of life for Black citizens in Tybee between 1912 and 1915. During that time, there were many suspicious fires that levelled houses, schools and churches in the district. Macon's police and firemen thought they were deliberate. On the evening of March 8, 1913, for example, five houses on Gilmer Street suddenly caught fire. Although no one was injured and the occupants were able to save their belongings, the houses were burned beyond repair.[69]

During 1914, there were twelve fires in the district over a ten-month period. One of these was the burning of the Black school on Turpin Street on Christmas morning. The wooden structure was almost completely destroyed before firemen were able to contain the blaze. The fire was not accidental. Kerosene-soaked packing material from a machine shop had been placed under pieces of weatherboarding and ignited. The fire chief stated that the arsonist "knew how to fire a building so that the walls and roof would ignite before the department could reach there." Five days later, another fire gutted S.P. Amerson's store in the same vicinity. As in the school burning, the fire department "believed it to have been of incendiary origin."[70]

But arson was just one form of violence that was used to terrorize Tybee's Black residents. On more than one occasion, Macon's White men resorted to vigilantism to send a message. That message was unmistakable in 1912 when White citizens learned that a Black man had attacked a White woman.

While walking home from work on the night of February 3, near Ocmulgee and First Street, a young White girl was pistol-whipped and sexually assaulted. A woman who lived near where the attack took place heard screams and opened her door. It was then that she saw a Black man, later identified as Charles Powell, dragging the girl down an embankment. She called the police, and Officers John Metts and Will Mosely were dispatched to the scene. As they approached Powell, he opened fire but failed to hit either officer. After a ferocious struggle, he was subdued and taken to police headquarters. It was soon learned that he had attempted to rape another woman in her home that same evening before escaping through a bedroom window.[71]

Macon authorities knew that once the public learned it was a Black man who had perpetrated the assault, there would be trouble. Hoping to avoid a lynching, they took Powell to the railroad yards and hid him in a boxcar with the intent of catching a train to Columbus or Atlanta. But acting on a tip from a railroad worker, a party of one hundred men found Powell's location and overpowered his guards. They dragged him, still handcuffed, out of the boxcar, tied him to a telephone pole and riddled his body with bullets.[72]

Powell's lynching did not placate many of Macon's White men. After learning that his corpse had been taken to an undertaker on Mulberry Street, a group of men broke into the establishment and loaded it into a delivery wagon. By then, well over three hundred men had gathered with the intention of burning the body on the premises. But believing this would be a good object lesson for the city's Black residents, the crowd followed the wagon to Tybee. It was there that a few men constructed a pyre with crossties and boxes doused with kerosene, while others ordered Blacks out of their homes to witness the cremation. As the fire reduced Powell's corpse to ashes, Tybee's Black citizens watched in horror, uncertain if the mob would suddenly turn on them. It didn't. The mob dispersed, satisfied that the message had been received.[73]

A similar message was sent in November 1919 when news came that a fifty-year-old White woman had been attacked by a Black man near the Central of Georgia railroad tracks as she returned home from church. Her assailant, later identified as Paul Jones, was soon captured and confined in a house in the Tybee District. It was not long before a mob formed and seized Jones from the deputies assigned to guard him. After the mob fired nearly fifty bullets into his body, they dragged him 150 yards down the Central of Georgia railroad tracks to a place where they then poured gasoline onto his body and set it on fire. No one was ever charged in Jones's lynching.[74]

Tybee's Black residents feared the worst when they heard news of the lynching of John Glover during the summer of 1922. On the afternoon of Saturday, July 29, Deputy Sheriff Walter C. Byrd and two other deputies went to Hatfield's poolroom on Broadway following up on a report that a Black man was threatening some of the patrons with a pistol. As the deputies entered the poolroom, the man, known to most as "Cocky" Glover, slipped past them. After exiting the building, the deputies saw Glover walking down the sidewalk and demanded that he stop. Glover turned and fired his pistol, hitting Byrd in the chest. The two other officers gave chase, but Glover, still firing, ran into the poolroom and escaped out the back window into the Tybee District. The officers returned to find Byrd dead and two Black men, Sam Brooks and George Marshall, seriously injured. Both would soon die from their wounds.[75]

News of the triple killing soon spread, and city officials prepared for the possibility of mob violence. Byrd was a tireless and accomplished officer who left behind a wife and two children. There was no way the city's White citizens were going to allow his death to go unavenged.

Not long after the shootings, a large number of men assembled on Broadway and began ransacking Black businesses and attacking Black citizens on the streets. Violence also erupted in other sections of the city. Some—acting on a rumor that C.H. Douglass, the owner of the Black theater, a hotel and a barbershop, had helped Glover elude the authorities— surrounded the businessman's house and threatened to kill him. Police, dispatched to the scene, were able to disperse the crowd before anyone was harmed.[76]

In a signed statement printed in the Macon *Telegraph*, Douglass denied emphatically that he had harbored Glover at one of his businesses. No one, he said, regretted the murder of the deputy more than he did. "Mr. Byrd was a good friend of mine and trusted me implicitly. I stand for law and order and teach my people the same."[77]

The search for Glover continued for several days until his capture on a Central of Georgia train in Spalding County. When a group of Macon men learned that deputies would be returning him to the city, they intercepted the party near Forsyth in Monroe County. The officers offered no resistance, even accompanying the crowd to the site where Glover was shot multiple times. His mutilated corpse was brought back to Macon and deposited in front of the Douglass Theater.[78]

Authorities in Bibb County vowed to bring those responsible for the lawlessness in Macon to justice and called a grand jury to investigate. After six weeks of hearing evidence, it failed to return any indictments. The policemen and curiosity seekers who witnessed the violence refused to name any of the perpetrators. For all Macon's citizens' pretensions to civility, said the grand jury, there was "sufficient proof of the lack of respect for law and authority in our midst, and should be a warning to us that our people have not been sufficiently taught to obey the law and respect authority." The grand jury had no other recourse but to conclude that the mob violence was done "by persons unknown."[79]

Chapter 4

A FLY IN THE OINTMENT

otwithstanding the bullying and intimidation, Tybee's residents, White and Black, continued business as usual with little notice from the city's moral and religious leaders—that is, until 1915. That year, Macon's ministers, angered by the city's toleration of open vice, began a campaign to close Tybee for good. As a result, from 1915 to 1917, a battle raged between the city's ministers and the mayor and city council over the future of Macon's segregated vice district.

Tybee's evolution as a protected red-light district alarmed the city's ministers as early as 1912. With brothels located on almost every street, prostitutes could be seen night and day conducting their business. The situation became so intolerable that the district's Black citizens proposed moving their churches and schools to more respectable areas.[80]

That Tybee's Black citizens would have to endure this constant humiliation, said W.N. Ainsworth, was appalling. But he was not surprised. He had lived in Macon for twenty years and had "never known it so wide open to the practice of shameless immorality as it is today." In a March 1913 sermon, Dr. Ainsworth blamed city officials. The mayor and the city council, he stated, were "fathering and fostering the culmination and spreading of crime, by encouraging the violation of decency and allowing the location of immoral women in this section of the city." Already a veteran of the war on saloons, he told Tybee's citizens to stand firm, and if no one else would act, he would. "Our young men are in peril in this city as never before. Let the slumbering citizens of our city awake."[81]

One citizen who took note of Dr. Ainsworth's call to action was Colonel Arthur Dasher, a candidate for the office of mayor in the fall of 1913. Seeking to embarrass the city administration, Dasher claimed that Mayor John Moore, the city council and prominent members of the business community had set up Tybee the previous year for financial gain. This "syndicate," as he called it, profited from the sale and leasing of real estate in the new restricted district. To protect their investment, the syndicate made sure that Tybee had fire protection and additional police officers and patrol wagons to maintain order, all at considerable cost to the city.[82]

While Dasher's claims did not resonate with voters, they did with the city's ministers. In a petition to the city council in March 1915, the Macon Ministerial Association demanded that it abolish the district. Tybee, they argued, degraded young men and perpetuated all forms of vice and political corruption.

The ministers further pointed out that they had given the subject of segregating vice much thought and study and had determined that it did not accomplish what it was intended to. Instead of containing prostitution, they argued, the district was responsible for the scattering of vice throughout the city. They estimated that there were three hundred professional lewd women in Macon and that only half worked in Tybee.[83]

The ministers' petition led to a heated debate among councilmen. Most argued that it was up to the Civil Service Commission to decide Tybee's fate. But Alderman Hay, who supported the ministers' call to close the district, believed his fellow councilmen were shirking their responsibilities. "They cannot get results from the civil service commission as to the Tybee district. This council created Tybee, and I was a party to it, and I am now sorry for it." Alderman Lee objected. "I resent the statement that we created Tybee," he declared, "and I would like for Alderman Hay to show me anything in the minutes that would make it appear so." Alderman Hay offered his apologies, stating that he "meant the mayor and council not particularly this mayor and council."[84]

The following Sunday, Macon's ministers took to their pulpits to denounce Tybee and the failure of city officials to close it. All agreed that Tybee was spreading vice and corruption all over the city. Tybee presented a constant temptation to men, said Reverend T.F. Callaway of the Tabernacle Baptist Church, and the only way to destroy the "social evil" and all other forms of vice was to eliminate any and all segregated districts. According to Reverend Callaway, segregated districts like Tybee encouraged whiskey drinking, gambling, lewd dancing and lust. "It was a

Macon's City Hall was the seat of local government since its construction in 1837. During the final months of the Civil War, however, it served as a temporary state capitol. Before World War I, it was the scene of many squabbles between the mayor, councilmen and ministers regarding the future of the red-light district. This photograph was taken in 1894. *Courtesy of Middle Georgia Archives, Washington Memorial Library.*

daily sight," he claimed, "to see young men go to the district in buggies and automobiles, fill them with the women of the underworld and ride around the district and into the country."[85]

Like Reverend Callaway, Dr. Ainsworth called attention to the growing number of young men who visited the district each day. "An average of 200 men and boys go nightly to these chambers of death. Ah! the strong men that are slain there. And the foolish youths that go like an ox to slaughter." For this, he said, the city officials and businessmen would have to face the judgment of the Almighty. "The curse of God is on the men in council and out of it who foisted upon this city the infamy of this district of disgrace. They are polluting the whole city's life."[86]

Reverend Leroy Anderson of First Christian Church chided the city for being a party to the steady exploitation of young women. "That hell hole," he said, referring to Tybee, "must be fed with new girls in the business and we are parties in the receiving of damaged goods." He saved his most stinging remarks for the men who profited from the trade. "When we begin to hit this business," he predicted, "a lot of these low down skunks who are wearing diamonds as big as a nut and are buying property with money which represents blood from these girls are going to yelp....We are talking of the fellows who are renting their property and receiving their rake-offs and anyone else financially interested in the business of selling a girl's person for a few cents." He assured his congregation that he was not afraid of the monied men who wanted to keep Tybee open. "Hell," he said, "would need a heating plant" before he would end his crusade.[87]

Despite the relentless pressure to close the district, the city council still insisted that the decision rested with the Civil Service Commission. In response, the commission stated that it could not act until the council repealed the ordinance establishing Tybee as a protected red-light district. But there was no such ordinance, only a directive from the mayor to the police that all disorderly houses be moved below Fifth Street. The council, consequently, decided in a seven-to-six vote to retain Tybee as the city's segregated district. Not wanting to be on record as supporting a district for lewd women, however, several councilmen changed their minds at the next meeting and voted to repeal the previous resolution.[88]

Yet this decision did nothing to change Tybee's status. Much to the disappointment of the ministers, the council still maintained that it had no actual power to close the district. Tybee's fate would be left to the Civil Service Commission.

While on record as opposing the operation of houses of ill fame in the city, both the members of the council and the commission feared the worst if the district was closed. It was widely known that Macon had the largest red-light district of any city of its size in the state. If it was suddenly shut down, where would its resident prostitutes go? The ministers believed that they would not scatter to other sections of the city. The people in most neighborhoods, they believed, would take legal action to keep them out.[89]

But many city officials, whether they chose to admit it publicly or not, were convinced that segregation was the best solution. Alderman Jones, for example, believed the ministers were ignorant of the situation and reproached them for not going into the district to help the women turn away from the profession. "I venture that there is not a minister here who has been down to see these women. Why if I was a minister I would love to go among sinners. Ministers can become mistaken the same as anyone else and I believe they know as little about this thing as anyone, for they do not go among them."[90]

For some sort of clue about what might happen in Macon if Tybee were closed, Alderman Jones and other members of the city council looked to what was unfolding in Atlanta. As in Macon, its officials were also under fire for allowing brothels in certain sections of the city.

Chapter 5

THE HOUSES IN OUR MIDST

tlanta in the early 1900s was a town fast on the move. It was not only Georgia's capital but also its largest and most diverse city. With businesses, factories and people from around the country locating there, it became a symbol of the New South. But like most cities of its size, it had several red-light districts that were permitted to operate as long as their residents confined their trade to a designated area. Better the city's scarlet women and brothels remain segregated, officials believed, than scatter throughout the city. But beginning in 1912, an organization of moral crusaders known as the Men and Religion Forward Movement put pressure on the mayor and council to do away with the protected vice districts. And with the help of ministers, politicians, newspapers and a supportive and enthusiastic police chief, it succeeded—but not without consequences. Many city officials and businessmen believed the movement and its champions had made the vice situation in Atlanta worse than before.[91]

The Men and Religion Forward Movement was national in scope and made up of middle-class urban men who wanted to make Protestant Christianity more muscular and forceful in addressing society's ills. While its leaders called attention to the many blind tigers and gambling joints in the city, its principal focus was on the rows of brothels that could be found along Manhattan Avenue and Mechanics and Collins Streets. It was in these houses of ill fame, under the willful protection of the city, they claimed, that pimps and madams exploited young girls.

MEN AND RELIGION BULLETIN No. 3

"The Houses in Our Midst"

Segregation a Failure
It Does Not Segregate

In Atlanta, the tree of Heaven, which offends the nostrils, is removed from our back yards and alleys by order of the Board of Health.

But the spread of the houses in our midst, the root of the evil deriving life from the seduction of girls and producing a harvest of blind eyes for innocent children and broken health and hearts for blameless wives—this is classed with the increase of banks and business enterprise as an evidence of our city's growth.

A Madame says the houses in Manhattan Avenue or Mechanic St., where a few weeks ago a man was killed in a drunken brawl—are better managed than those in other cities.

Doubtless the same experienced judge would consent to select a committee of citizens, to whom should be entrusted the selection of the pure girls to be betrayed to make fallen women, the stock in trade of the houses in our midst, these so well conducted houses in our segregated district.

This district of which our disinterested critic speaks so highly has demonstrated that segregation does not segregate.

Witness the presence of forty-four houses and the social evil in many hotels and assignation houses in our city.

Our experience is identical with that of other cities which have tried this system that even Berlin, Paris and Vienna, with legalized prostitution, will not attempt.

Toledo and Cleveland are usually referred to as models of segregation, yet their chiefs of police advised the Minneapolis Vice Commission not to establish a Red Light District.

The evidence before that commission showed that, despite segregation, assignation houses are in operation in Cleveland and "women of shady reputation are scattered through the city in flats and other places."

The assistant chief of police of Des Moines made the following statement: "In the days of the 'Red Light' District, when it was commonly supposed that lewd women were segregated, not more than 15 per cent of the traffic was really carried on in the district. Everywhere in the city were disorderly houses. It was impossible to control them."

Cincinnati has the segregated district. With reference to it the following appears in the report of the Vice Commission of Minneapolis: "The result has been that all kinds of degradation have been developed within the so-called 'Red Light District' and women and men have been allowed to conduct houses of assignation all over the city. 'The white slaver' has his headquarters in the most select neighborhoods; and the best restaurants, places of amusement and even schools and conservatories have been hunting grounds of the procuresses."

Sunday, go to the House of God. Hear His word. Then think of the houses in our midst and ask not man, but your conscience, in the light of the teachings of Jesus Christ, what you, as a citizen sharing your city's shame, should do with reference to this unspeakable commerce in the souls and bodies of women!

THE EXECUTIVE COMMITTEE
Of the Men and Religion Forward Movement

(To Be Continued)

The Men and Religion Forward Movement regularly published bulletins entitled "The Houses in Our Midst" in the Atlanta newspapers. Each one attacked the city's businessmen and government officials for protecting and profiting from the red-light district. *Courtesy of the Atlanta Constitution.*

The Atlanta organization clearly had resources. Between 1912 and 1915, it hired detectives and self-styled experts on the sex trade to investigate conditions in the city's brothels. It also published a long series of bulletins in the city's newspapers alerting the public to the social evil and attacking government officials for doing nothing to stop it. Each bulletin was numbered and entitled "The Houses in Our Midst."

In explicit language, the authors described Atlanta as a place where White slavers and those who protected them got rich. According to bulletin no. 5, the city's brothels were raking in $700,000 each year buying and selling young girls. But it was Atlanta's landlords who gained the most. As in other cities, they were able to get higher rent for their houses in the segregated districts than in other neighborhoods.[92]

The same bulletin called to task those who claimed that the vice was segregated in these districts and did not impact the rest of the city. This, they said, was an "unbearable pretense." Prostitutes had set up shop in hotels, residential neighborhoods and the business district. Segregation had not segregated. On the contrary, it had emboldened the city's harlots to ply their trade wherever they thought it most profitable.[93]

The movement's portrayal of Atlanta as a Sodom and Gomorrah angered the business community. As a consequence, some called out its leaders for sensationalizing the issue and defaming the city's reputation. "These misguided men of the so-called 'religion movement,'" said Benjamin M. Blackburn in an open letter to the *Atlanta Georgian*, "have already advertised Atlanta to the world, as a city reeking in moral filth, and honey-combed with hidden crime—injuring her status in moral estimate beyond compare, hurting her financial future to an incalculable degree; embarrassing her civic pride in an unspeakable sense." A week later, in another letter to the same paper, he maintained that the movement's leaders were doing little to promote morality. According to Blackburn, their coarse and graphic descriptions of the sex trade piqued the interest of the prurient and offended the sensibilities of the respectable.[94]

Colonel Frederic J. Paxon, a retail merchant, stated in December 1913 that the bulletins had "created the impression throughout the country that Atlanta is the most vice-ridden city on earth." Parents who had read the bulletins, said Paxon, were now reconsidering sending their children to Atlanta schools out of fear that they might fall victim to the social evil.

Speaking of children, the bulletins, he argued, did not teach boys and girls the lessons that they intended. Instead, children regarded them "merely as salacious morsels of reading, and a discussion of forbidden subjects, clothed in repulsive, yet fascinating language." Young people found them alluring and waited eagerly for the next bulletin to appear. Girls as well as boys, he had observed, discussed their contents openly. Some even cut them out of the papers to share with friends.[95]

With few exceptions, bankers, real estate men, company executives and politicians tended to agree with Paxon and Blackburn. Some believed that the movement had gone far enough in its criticism. Forest Adair, a real estate investor, stated in a newspaper interview that the sensational but unsupported stories about White slavery had done great damage, causing many outsiders to hesitate before bringing their families to the city to live. "Every time a man is caught with an old and faded woman on the streets it is termed a case of 'White slavery' until the public is disgusted." Much of what was contained in the bulletins, he said, was just "tommyrot," referring to a story that there were "needle men" hunting for young women to drug and kidnap in the city's theaters. He welcomed the day when the city "returned to a condition of sanity."[96]

CHIEF OF POLICE JAMES L. BEAVERS.
Who will be tried by police board on Thursday night on four charges.

Atlanta chief of police James L. Beavers championed the closure of Atlanta's red-light district. It eventually would cost him his job. *Courtesy of the* Atlanta Constitution.

But the movement had a champion in James L. Beavers, the newly appointed chief of police. From the moment he took office in 1912, Beavers focused his department's efforts on closing the city's most infamous red-light district, which was located on Manhattan Avenue. His motive, he maintained in an interview, was not to head a moral crusade but simply to uphold the law. "I looked at it from all angles; I considered it from everybody's standpoint. But after all there was the law. And what right had I, as chief of police, to say to these women, 'You can live and ply your trade in this street, but not in that; you must not come next door to my house, but you may go to Manhattan Avenue.' I had no such right; no man had such right."[97]

By the spring of 1913, Beavers had succeeded in closing the brothels along Manhattan Avenue as well as those in other, less visible vice districts in the city. Atlanta, he believed, was now a cleaner city. In fact, at the annual convention of the International

Association of Police Chiefs, he maintained that there was not one brothel still operating in the city. "The closing of the district," he added, "has had the effect of decreasing crime and disorder fully one-third, which fact alone shows the wisdom of this decision." He later reiterated this claim in a letter to the National Mayor's Conference in Auburn, New York, in 1914. Streetwalkers and assignation houses, he wrote, had all been "wiped away, as they know the police are watching them."[98]

Beavers's decision, however, did not sit well with many city officials and businessmen. They feared, perhaps with good reason, that once the district was closed, prostitutes and brothels would move their trade into neighborhoods throughout the city. Many who had invested in property and businesses in and around the red-light district also stood to lose quite a bit of money. Houses that would ordinarily rent for $100 per month in some of the more fashionable neighborhoods brought $600 to $800 per month in the area along Manhattan Avenue.[99]

Beavers's crusade, however, won the applause of the movement and most of the churches in the city. Thanks to Chief Beavers, said Reverend John E. White of the Second Baptist Church, Atlanta was "the cleanest, finest, most progressive moral community of 200,000 people in the Republic and getting better each day for boys and girls to live in." Marion Jackson, the head of the movement's executive committee and author of many of its bulletins, heaped praise on the chief for taking on what he believed was a partnership between city officials and the men who profited from the red-light district: "The favored few were growing rich 'by special privilege' that of operating in the so-called district. Rightly, the Chief began with this, the worst and most foul nest of crime in our city. He ended it."[100]

But many Atlantans were coming to believe that the chief's decisions were not of his own making. An editorial in the Macon *Telegraph* argued that Beavers, under the influence of Marion Jackson, had succeeded only in spreading prostitution throughout the city. "Immoral women infest every corner and nook in Atlanta like the dust that gathers in the corners. There was a time when a man had to seek them out to find them in the Capital of the State. Now they seek him and hunt him out; on every curb, in every café the smile of the siren is seen, always playing to a definite purpose. Atlanta has begun to privately admit that a terrible mistake was made."[101]

By early 1915, city officials, especially Mayor James G. Woodward, had come to agree that Beavers had gone too far. Closing Atlanta's red-light district had done nothing to clean up the city. The problem was worse than before. Each day, he received complaints about houses of ill fame doing

MR. JAMES G. WOODWARD, four times mayor of Atlanta and one of the most picturesque figures in the city's political history, who died late Wednesday afternoon at a private sanitarium. He was seventy-eight years old.

MARION M. JACKSON
Well known attorney, who is one of the leading spirits in the Men and Religion Forward Movement.

Left: Marion Jackson was the mastermind behind the Men and Religion Forward Movement's bulletins. *Courtesy of the* Atlanta Journal.

Right: Atlanta mayor James G. Woodward openly sparred with Chief Beavers, believing his crusade against the red-light district had led to the scattering of prostitutes throughout the city. *Courtesy of the* Atlanta Journal.

business in respectable neighborhoods. Once more, murders, robberies and assaults were at an unprecedented level. Beavers's crusade against houses of prostitution, many believed, had left the city vulnerable.[102]

The police board decided to create a special committee to investigate the situation. Police officers who testified before the committee all claimed that prostitution was now far worse than before. Prostitutes in brothels and streetwalkers, they said, could be found plying their trade in the business district and in most neighborhoods of the city. On the recommendation of the committee, the board decided to demote Beavers to captain and replace him with his subordinate, Captain W.H. Mayo. The humiliation was too much for the former chief, and he quit the force.[103]

Not surprisingly, there was a backlash from the movement and the city's churches. Beavers, they stated, was a man of strong moral convictions who had done his best to enforce the law. In a majority of the city's churches, ministers denounced the board's decision. Beavers's only failing, in their view, was that his closing of the red-light district took money out of the pockets of those who owned property there. And in an effort to return the chief to his former position, the Atlanta Association of Baptist Churches called for the unseating of the seven commissioners who had voted to remove him.[104]

These efforts, however, made little headway. While the red-light district along Manhattan Avenue remained officially closed, the city's prostitutes and brothels still did business there and in other parts of the city unabated. By 1916, city officials returned to a policy of allowing houses of ill fame to operate within restricted areas of the city. But this would not last long. The approach of World War I would force both Atlanta and Macon to close their protected red-light districts.

Chapter 6

FIT TO FIGHT

*A*s city officials watched prostitutes scatter throughout Atlanta, they became convinced that closing Tybee would be a mistake. But as the country drew closer to entering the war in Europe in 1917, it became clear they could do little to keep it open. The War Department was set to impose health regulations on all cities with military camps nearby. With Camp Wheeler and Camp Harris located just outside the city, Macon would come under government scrutiny. The Tybee District would have to be closed, said the War Department, in order to protect soldiers from venereal disease.

The decision was informed by what generals and medical personnel had witnessed during the Civil War. According to the *Medical and Surgical History of the War of the Rebellion*, among White troops, there "were reported 73,382 cases of syphilis and 109,397 cases of gonorrhea." This indicated that there was an annual rate of 82 cases per 1,000 men for all types of venereal disease. The incidence of infection among Black troops was lower, with 34 cases of syphilis and 44 cases of gonorrhea per year per 1,000 men.[105]

While there are no accurate records of the cases of venereal infection among Confederate troops other than the antidotal evidence found in soldiers' letters and diaries, historians generally believe that the rate was low. Unlike Confederate armies, Federal forces were often encamped in or near small towns and cities and had more opportunities for assignations with prostitutes. These "public women," as they were called, could be found in large numbers in red-light districts in the urban South. Historian

Catherine Clinton states, for example, that during its occupation, Nashville had over 1,500 prostitutes, many of them infected with syphilis and gonorrhea, who worked the streets and brothels in an area of the city known as Smokey Row.[106]

The presence of so many diseased prostitutes in Nashville, Memphis, New Orleans and other occupied cities could have a devastating impact on an army's ability to keep soldiers healthy. Syphilis and gonorrhea left soldiers fatigued, with severe muscle and joint pain, rashes, ulcers, pus-like discharge from the eyes and swollen lymph nodes. Infected soldiers rarely developed more serious symptoms, but they generally were rendered useless on the battlefield.[107]

At the time of the Civil War, there was no effective treatment for venereal diseases. As early as the sixteenth century, physicians had experimented with mercury in various forms to delay the progress of syphilis. Often used topically to treat skin diseases, mercury, many believed, could be applied as an ointment to the ulcers that were associated with syphilis. More commonly, mercury was administered orally or used in steam baths. This practice was based on the theory that the salivation and perspiration caused by the combination of the chemical and hot vapors would draw out the poisonous humors in the body and restore good health.[108]

The treatment provided little or no relief from the ravages of the disease and, in fact, did more harm than good. Patients developed painful mouth sores, loss of teeth, kidney failure and hemorrhaging of the bowel. Despite the side effects, doctors continued this approach and were not inclined to seek other remedies. The prevailing attitude was that syphilis patients would have to suffer for their sins. "A night with Venus," so went the saying, "and a lifetime with mercury."

But by the early 1900s, the spread of the disease through the ranks of the middle and upper classes had brought about a change in attitudes, and Progressive reformers in the United States initiated a social hygiene movement to address matters of sexuality. This led to a more scientific approach to sexually transmitted diseases. Researchers in Germany discovered a way to determine whether a patient's lesions were caused by syphilis or some other condition. This was groundbreaking; no longer would diagnosis of the disease be based on the subjective judgment of the physician.[109]

In 1909, a breakthrough in treatment occurred when immunologists Paul Erlich and Sahachiro Hata discovered an arsenic-based drug that ameliorated the effects of syphilis. Later marketed as Salvarsan, the drug became the most widely used treatment for the disease. Unfortunately, it

Before the discovery of Salvarsan in 1909, syphilis was treated, albeit ineffectively, with mercury. *Courtesy of the Library of Congress.*

required intravenous injections on a regular basis, and many patients suffered from the side effects of large doses of arsenic.[110]

Despite the discovery of Salvarsan, the most effective way to keep America's fighting men disease-free and in fighting form, the War Department asserted, was to make sure soldiers and seamen had no contact with prostitutes. As a consequence, Macon and other cities with army encampments or naval bases (including Atlanta, Columbus, Augusta and Savannah) would have to shut down their red-light districts.

The *Macon News*, which had long denounced the Tybee District, encouraged all citizens to support the government's action. "The law is perfectly clear," said the *News*. "No such places are to be tolerated within five miles of any army camp or military post of any nature." The restricted district, it said, should be "cleaned up without the slightest delay."[111]

But shutting down Tybee, as John Hammond of the Macon *Telegraph*'s Atlanta bureau argued in a June 1917 editorial, was not going to keep lewd women away from soldiers. After Chief Beavers shut down Manhattan Avenue, prostitutes took up residence in every form of housing available in the city. "Apartment life in Atlanta, in many instances," he observed, "has suffered the contamination of the 'Vice Crusade.' Some of the handsomest and most desirable of that class of property has been tainted beyond acceptance of risk by people. Residential districts are infected in spots all over Atlanta."[112]

A recent fire in a residential area revealed the extent of the problem. Families left homeless in the aftermath found it difficult to find suitable housing and neighborhoods to raise their children. "There were, the day after the conflagration, two or three thousand vacant residence buildings in Atlanta of varying grades of desirability. Dozens upon dozens of them were attractive in arrangement and appearance, but investigation brought out the fact that they were 'on a pretty bad block' and, therefore, impossible for family use."[113]

Things were only going to get worse. The establishment of two army camps nearby would bring seventy-five to eighty thousand men to the city. Seeing opportunity, a large number of new professional women would soon follow. He estimated that with at least one prostitute for every twenty men, the city could expect an influx of four thousand lewd women into the city. And where would they live? Not wanting to attract the attention of the police, they would not congregate in one area but would scatter to neighborhoods, boardinghouses, apartments and hotels all over the city. This, he said, was "food for thought" for Macon.[114]

But Macon city officials had no choice. The United States District Attorney, under direction of the War Department, ordered that Tybee be closed. Although city's officials believed this to be a mistake, they fully cooperated. All people operating houses of ill fame would be prosecuted under sections 1093 and 1094 of the city code. Those who chose to continue

Named for Confederate lieutenant general Joseph Wheeler, Camp Wheeler was established as an army training camp in 1917. During World War I, it reached a troop strength of 28,960. *Courtesy of the Georgia Historical Society.*

their trade in the district would be "given the privilege of either leaving the city or standing trial."[115]

What city's officials feared, however, came true when Tybee officially closed on September 1. Instead of leaving the city, prostitutes moved their trade to hotels, boardinghouses, residential neighborhoods and the business district. Seeking assignations with soldiers at Camp Harris and Camp Wheeler, a new class of prostitutes from outside Middle Georgia also now joined Macon's professional women. The city's vice problem had exploded.[116]

On October 24, the Civil Service Commission met with Alan Johnstone Jr., special agent for the Federal Commission on Training Camp Activities, to discuss the vice problem. According to Johnstone, secret agents had reported to him that conditions were worse than before the closing of the district. Something had to be done—and done quickly.[117]

The city attorney asked Johnstone what sort of plan should be adopted. The special agent said that the city would have to get more aggressive in its efforts. Macon's officials, however, said that the police were doing everything possible to repress prostitution in the city. "But you are not getting results," said Johnstone. "There is not a hotel in Macon which has not had lewd women in it since the first investigation," he declared, "and street solicitation has grown worse to an alarming degree." Compared to other cities with military camps, Macon was failing to protect soldiers from prostitutes.[118]

The commander of Camp Wheeler, Brigadier General J.L. Hayden, believed that if the chief of police was given a free hand, prostitutes would be forced to find residence elsewhere. But the police department, said the Civil Service Commission, faced an uphill battle. Since the opening of the two camps, the number of prostitutes had doubled. Once more, they had scattered to every corner of the city. The problem was compounded, the commission said, by the fact that police officers were well known to them, making it difficult to gain enough evidence to make an arrest.[119]

Representatives from Macon's Hotel Association expressed similar frustration. They knew, as agent Johnstone said, that their establishments were infested with lewd women. But trying to keep them out was a challenge. Prostitutes and their clients used every possible ruse to gain admittance.[120]

The Macon Chamber of Commerce and the Rotary Club decided that the problem was beyond the control of the police and the hotel managers. It was time for public-spirited citizens to act. On October 26, the two organizations called a special joint meeting of ministers, laymen, military officers, medical personnel and city officials. Without one dissent, all present supported a resolution to create "a committee of fifty to hunt out the women and to employ others to find them and drive them out of the city." The resolution also called on the federal government to provide secret agents to help with the search.[121]

The superintendent of the Camp Wheeler hospital said it was imperative that they act immediately. Medical records indicated that almost 2 percent of the men there were infected with venereal disease. But recently, he added, there was an alarming trend, with new cases among the men rising at a rate of ten per day.[122]

There was good reason to be concerned. Just two days earlier, Josephus Daniels, secretary of the navy, had addressed the issue before the Clinical Congress of Surgeons of North America. According to Daniels, venereal disease posed as great a threat to soldiers and seamen as machine guns and cannon. "There is not an army in the field whose effectiveness is not reduced by reason of immoral disease," said the secretary. Speaking of those under his own command, he said, "The navy suffers likewise and business halts because venereal diseases destroy the manhood of workmen and fathers. During the last statistical year men of the American navy lost 141,378 days sickness from a small group of absolutely preventable diseases, or rather diseases contracted by sin."[123]

The secretary believed that the only solution was for the medical profession to take a proactive approach and tell young people about the ravages of sexually transmitted diseases. "Tell our youths the truth. It is a duty laid upon you, not by the moral law alone, but by the law of self-preservation that operates in nations as well as individuals." The nation's physicians had no other recourse, he contended, but to give soldiers and sailors wise counsel.

In doing this, they would "contribute more to the winning of the war than manufacturers of shells."[124]

The unfortunate reality at Camp Wheeler, however, was that warnings about the dangers of venereal infection were having little effect. The temptations available to young men were far too great to resist. Prostitutes could be found anywhere in Macon. And with the aid of taxicab drivers, waiters and bellhops, soldiers could easily arrange sexual encounters with any class of professional woman that they desired. The only way to protect young soldiers and keep them "fit to fight," concluded officials, was for police, federal agents and patriotic citizens to hunt down and drive prostitutes from the city.[125]

Chapter 7

AN IMPROMPTU UNDERWORLD

*D*espite their best efforts, Macon's officials and vigilantes struggled to rid the city of prostitution and other forms of vice after the closing of Tybee. Vigorous policing, surveillance and more arrests seemed to accomplish little or nothing. There was much money to be made in sex, gambling, blind tigers and bootleg whiskey, and the rewards far outweighed the risks. By the end of World War I, the denizens of Macon's underworld had created an impromptu culture of vice that the city found almost impossible to break.

By January 1919, the situation had grown so bad that Miss Evelyn Williams of the Federal Law Enforcement Department for Women and Girls, together with U.S. public health officers and the city's ministers, called on the Civil Service Commission to take "drastic steps" to clean up the city. Speaking before a special meeting of the city council, Williams claimed that prostitutes had practically taken over the city's streets and that a new red-light district was starting to develop. She blamed the police:

> *The vice problem is growing so serious we must have some arrests. There has been a "slump" in the activity of the police along these lines. The city managers must give us more cooperation. I know where the immoral houses are and who the women are. Immoral women are not on the streets by the dozen, but by the hundreds. There is a persistent rumor that the red-light district is to be opened again, but we must not tolerate that.* [126]

Madams, she said, were now operating brothels along Broadway. One of them was well known for its steady business. "On the 700 block on Broadway, there is a certain house where fifteen girls are housed. Taxicab drivers are in the habit of going to this place at night and signaling these women from a brick building on the opposite side of the street."[127]

The city, she said, had at least three to four hundred known prostitutes, but it was difficult to get their names. Many had at least thirty or so aliases. This, however, was no excuse for not arresting them. "Any man knows a lewd woman on the streets when he sees her. Names mean nothing."[128] Nevertheless, she promised to provide the names of prostitutes and a list of the disorderly houses in the city, including boardinghouses and hotels, to the Civil Service Commission at its next meeting. But Williams never appeared or sent the names.[129]

In the meantime, a row occurred over reports that the Civil Service Commission was considering reopening Tybee. The commission vehemently denied the reports as mere rumors intended to embarrass its members who were running for reelection. "Tybee shall not come back," declared commissioner Julian Urquhart. "If it does exist now in Macon, I am sure no member of the civil service commission knows of it or approves of it, but would do everything in his power to wipe it off even the old Macon map."[130]

But even if the commission had no intention of reopening the old district, there was no denying that prostitutes were establishing little red-light districts in every section of the city. According to Mayor Glen Toole, "Instead of one Tybee in Macon, there are now ten."[131] The commission, in response, ordered police officers to increase their surveillance of suspected disorderly houses. In order to assist them in their investigations, the city council passed a boardinghouse ordinance. Officers would now have the authority to demand the names and places of business of all occupants.

These efforts appeared to yield results. Beginning in 1920, Macon's newspapers reported numerous arrests of women for keeping disorderly houses. Many of the arrests were in the area near Tybee along Broadway. Others took place on Third, Pine, Mulberry, Plum, Oak, Maple, Ocmulgee and Forsyth Streets.

Many of the women who ran brothels out of their boardinghouses became well known to the police. Mollie Burgamy, for example, made frequent appearances before the court both prior to and after World War I. Between 1916 and her death at the age of sixty-seven in 1926, she was arrested countless times for keeping lewd houses in Tybee and in other areas of the city and violating the prohibition laws.[132] Like Mollie, Mrs. C.L.

Snyers, who ran a boardinghouse on the corner of Mulberry and Broadway, was in and out of court between 1920 and 1922 for operating a lewd house. Mary Jackson and Mrs. W.B. Bullock (a.k.a. Fritzi Strauss) regularly flouted the law and were charged with operating lewd houses in various sections of East Macon between 1922 and 1924.[133]

Managers of the city's hotels often found themselves at odds with the vice laws. Harry Griggs, who owned the Saratoga Hotel on Mulberry Street, was repeatedly arrested for operating a lewd house. In 1922, city authorities declared his hotel a nuisance and ordered him to vacate the premises. Eventually, he was able to get an injunction preventing the city's order on the grounds that he was never given a fair hearing. A year later, however, Griggs was convicted of running a lewd house and sentenced to the county chain gang. But he had friends in high places. Governor Hardwick, on the recommendation of trial jurors, police officers and prominent citizens, commuted his sentence. He paid a $250 fine and was released.[134]

While Harry renamed his hotel the Eagle, he made no effort to stay out of trouble. In 1926, he was sentenced to a year in the federal penitentiary for violating the prohibition laws. This came after he was found guilty of trying to bribe Will Faulk of Eastman to testify against state prohibition agents on his behalf. According to Faulk, Griggs said he would furnish him with a room and all the whiskey, money and women he wanted. The judge in the case was not amused and ordered the Eagle Hotel padlocked for a period of twelve months.

Harry Griggs was just one of many men in Macon who saw opportunity with the adoption of prohibition. With saloons, restaurants and hotels not

Illegal drinking establishments called speakeasies or blind tigers like this one carefully scrutinized each customer who sought entry. *Courtesy of the American Prohibition Museum.*

With the adoption of prohibition, women, who had previously been barred from saloons by city ordinance, now drank with men in Macon's numerous blind tigers and speakeasies. *Courtesy of the American Prohibition Museum.*

allowed to serve alcohol, enterprising men and women found ways to give the public what it wanted. As a result, a subculture of blind tigers, speakeasies and back-alley shot houses developed. This, together with the constant flood of bootleg liquor into the homes of the city's best families, as well as the brothels, made Macon the place to go for a drink and a good time.

And having a good time was all the rage in the 1920s. Jazz music and dances like the Charleston, coupled with cocktails and cigarettes, could be found in secret clubs and private parties in every section of the city. Men and women alike eschewed Victorian morality and embraced the latest fashions in dress, mannerisms and social attitudes.[135]

But it was prohibition, strangely enough, that was breaking down the barriers of Victorianism in Macon and other cities. Before its adoption, women in the city were not permitted in saloons or hotel bars. Yet with all such establishments banned from serving alcohol, women found that they could drink with men in places that operated outside the law. This was a turning point. Women were now accepted into the traditionally masculine world of drinking, and after the repeal of prohibition, they, just like men, would be allowed to patronize public bars and saloons.

Illicit sex and illegal alcohol, however, were just one part of Macon's underworld in the 1920s. Gambling, though long tolerated, was singled out as a vice that threatened to destroy the moral and spiritual well-being of the city. Before the war, Macon's ministers had initiated a campaign to break up card and craps games as well as the more sophisticated numbers and lottery rackets that pervaded the city. But by using stores, poolrooms, restaurants and hotels as fronts for their operations, the heads of the city's underworld of gambling managed to evade detection and arrest. And even in those cases when they were discovered, police officers could do little but confiscate cards, dice, roulette wheels and any other paraphernalia associated with the vice. Few were ever convicted.

Chapter 8

MURDER AND WHISKEY ON SWIFT CREEK ROAD

On Monday, July 12, 1926, G.L. Cobb, a farmer and well-known bootlegger in the Swift Creek section of Bibb County, walked down Camp Wheeler Road, which ran near his home. With him were Bars Davis, Joe Bonner and A.E. Odom. They were searching for traces of blood. Davis, Cobb's farmhand and partner in the liquor trade, had told them that morning that he had seen blood on the side of the road and that maybe they should investigate. Cobb had not been concerned until he learned that his neighbor G.C. Bonner, Joe's brother, had been missing since Saturday night. He thought about what Davis had told him and decided that he and his neighbors should see for themselves.[136]

The party found a trail of blood leading from a thicket to a parked Ford Roadster deep in the woods. It was on the passenger's side of the vehicle that they found the bodies of a young man and woman lying on the ground. They had been shotgunned at close range.[137]

Sheriff J.L. Hicks and deputies arrived on the scene and determined that the couple were E.W. Wilson, twenty-one, and Hilda Smith, twenty. Wilson had been shot behind his right ear. The blast had torn much of his head away. Miss Smith had been shot through her left ear and her left hand. Apparently, she had attempted to shield herself from the shot. Like Wilson, she had powder burns on both her hand and head. They both had been shot at point-blank range. The car was covered in blood, and there were two holes in the roof made by a shotgun.[138]

E.W., who worked at his brother's dairy and lived with his father, Joseph, in the Cross Keys section of the county, had been seeing Hilda for a year. Hilda worked as a clerk for the Union Dry Goods Company in Macon and lived at the YWCA dormitory. She was, as Mary M. Milner, the director of the facility, said, well loved and considered by her friends "the ideal girl." Milner also had high praise for E.W. and was delighted to learn that the couple were to be married. Friends, coworkers and family members said that they had no enemies. Why would anyone want to do them harm?[139]

Hilda Smith and her fiancé, E.W. Wilson, were murdered in July 1926 in their rented Ford Roadster on Swift Creek Road outside of Macon. *Courtesy of the Macon Telegraph.*

Sheriff Hicks's investigation discovered just how the couple came to be in the Swift Creek area the night they were shot. According to E.W.'s father, E.W. told him on Saturday, July 10, that he wanted to take Hilda for a ride. Although he did not own a vehicle, he frequently rented one. He was in high spirits and went to Macon to lease a Ford Roadster from the Drive-It Company for the evening. Soon after, he picked up Hilda at her dormitory and drove five miles to the Camp Wheeler Road. Tire tracks in the vicinity of where they were found indicated that the car was probably parked when they were shot.[140]

The location of the shooting was very close to the site where A.H. Byars, a traveling salesman for the Morris Company, had been mortally wounded in 1921. Viola Brewer, who was with him at the time, said that he had stopped the car to adjust the headlights. Just as he closed the hood, he was hit with a blast from a shotgun. Seeing that he was seriously wounded, Brewer jumped from the car and, after walking some distance, was able to flag down an approaching vehicle. Byars was taken to the hospital in Macon, where he died two days later.[141]

Sheriff Hicks compared the Byars shooting to that of E.W. and Hilda. In both cases, the victims had been killed in approximately the same geographic area by a shotgun blast at close range. And all three had been out joyriding with their lovers when they were gunned down. Was this a coincidence, or were the three murders linked?[142]

Hicks was uncertain. But what he did know was that the area where E.W. and Hilda were found was the most notorious moonshining district in the

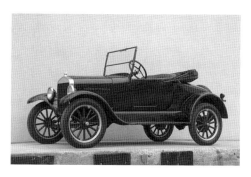

Pictured is a 1926 Ford Roadster like the one E.W. Wilson rented in Macon for a country drive with Hilda the evening they were murdered. *Courtesy of the Smithsonian Museum.*

county. In fact, near the scene of the crime, one hundred gallons of whiskey and a still had just been discovered. Were G.L. Cobb, Bars Davis and others who trafficked in liquor somehow involved? The sheriff found no evidence connecting them to the crime. But with the uncovering of their liquor operations, they would be charged and eventually convicted of violating state and federal prohibition laws.[143]

Hicks's suspicions now turned to Ed Glover, a Black man who had been seen in the area carrying a single-barreled shotgun. During questioning, Glover confessed to the crime. Additional questioning of Alberta Pitts, with whom Glover occasionally stayed at the Royster Guano Company quarters, revealed the whereabouts of articles of clothing and a watch that he had taken from the couple. Glover admitted that he had taken an umbrella, a lady's hat, a man's hat and a watch and left them with Alberta Pitts. Fearful that he would be found out, he burned everything except the watch, which he hid in some brush not too far from the scene of the killing.[144]

But what was the motive? At first, Glover explained that he had been hunting rabbits when he came across the couple parked on the side of the road. When E.W. saw him, he yelled for Hilda to get his gun. Fearful that the young man was going to shoot him, he opened fire, killing both E.W. and Hilda with two blasts.[145]

As the sheriff would later discover, this was not, in fact, how Glover came to kill the couple. In a full confession, Glover stated that on Saturday, July 10, 1926, he left his home in the Swift Creek section of Bibb County for the farm of G.L. Cobb. His mission that evening was to get some whiskey from Bars Davis, who boarded with Cobb. Davis, Cobb and Floy Cobb Lee, G.L.'s daughter, made and sold whiskey to people in Macon as well as the farmers and farmhands who lived in the vicinity. It was common knowledge that anyone could purchase liquor from them day or night.[146]

Davis had been drinking and was in a foul mood. E.W. had just been there asking for liquor. Davis refused him and demanded that E.W. pay him for what he had already purchased from him on credit. E.W. didn't have the money and insisted that he would pay Davis later if Davis would just let him have a gallon. Davis was adamant: "Pay me now." The argument grew heated, and E.W. left without his liquor.[147]

Later, according to Glover, Davis asked to borrow his 16-gauge shotgun. He wanted to kill the young man. E.W., Davis said, owed him a lot of money for whiskey. Glover refused to relinquish his weapon. But Davis, Glover claimed, said he would give Glover twenty-five dollars and a gallon of whiskey if he would do the deed. Still reluctant, Davis then pulled a pistol and told Glover that if he didn't agree to shoot Wilson, he would kill him.[148]

Convinced that Davis was serious, Glover went with him down an embankment and through a barbed-wire fence near G.L. Cobb's home. Crawling through the woods, they came within a few feet of the car. Davis said that they were close enough and told Glover to fire. But before he could do so, Hilda saw him and shouted, "There's an old negro." E.W. then turned, demanded to know what Glover was doing there and shouted to Hilda to get his pistol. Glover fired but missed. He then reloaded and, this time, shot E.W. in the head. Glover did not intend to kill Hilda, but just as he fired, she threw herself in front of her fiancé in an effort to protect him from the blast.[149]

Glover stated that he and Davis put the bodies in the car and drove into the woods. They then laid E.W. and Hilda on the ground. Hilda, he said, groaned; she was not yet dead. They then collected a number of items, including three dollars from Hilda's purse, and fled the scene.[150]

News of the killing and Glover's confession spread through Macon and Bibb County. There was talk of a lynching, but the sheriff made it clear that no one was going to take Glover from the county jail. More curious than violent, a large crowd gathered outside the jail. The sheriff, however, was not taking any chances. He had a large coterie of men armed with anti-riot gear to stop any attempt to seize Glover. There would be no lynching in Macon.[151]

Glover never wavered from his story. Davis, he said, was angry that E.W. had refused to pay his debt. Drunk and determined to get his due in blood, he ordered Glover to kill the young man if he wanted to live. Nevertheless, Glover was found guilty of first-degree murder and sentenced to die in the electric chair in the state prison in Milledgeville.[152]

Although Davis acknowledged that he had initially given some misinformation to county authorities to protect his liquor business, he maintained that he had nothing to do with the killings. A jury thought otherwise; Glover's testimony was consistent and compelling. Davis was found guilty of accessory to murder. He was sentenced to life in prison.[153]

The scene in Milledgeville during the days leading up to Glover's execution on September 9, 1926, was poignant. Ministers and Christian workers prayed and sang hymns with him in his cell. Glover told them that he had faith in God and that he believed he was forgiven of his sins. But while Glover found peace in the assurance that he would have a place in heaven, he felt that it wasn't right that he was being made to pay the ultimate price for a crime that Davis instigated. It "ain't fair for me to have to go unless Mr. Davis goes too," he said. "He is more guilty than I is."[154]

The morning of the execution, Glover stated that he had gotten a good night's sleep and that he "was ready to go." He was then led to the execution chamber and seated in the chair that would take his life. As the hood was pulled over his eyes, he asked that it be quick. "Please don't burn me," he said. He then asked the ministers present to sing a couple of hymns. They granted his wish and sang "His Eyes Are Upon the Sparrow" and "Nearer My God to Thee." After they finished, the signal was given to the electrician to pull the switch. It took three shots of current before Ed could be pronounced dead.[155]

While Sheriff Hicks could take some degree of satisfaction in solving the murders of E.W. and Hilda, the mystery of A.H. Byars's killing still remained. Was he, too, the victim of a liquor deal gone wrong, or was he perhaps a victim of mistaken identity? Worse yet, could he have been just a random target of someone's bloodlust? Unfortunately, the sheriff would never know. The Byars killing was never solved.

Chapter 9

A CALL TO ARMS

The brutality of the Swift Creek Road murders shocked the Macon community. Something had to be done about the traffic in bootleg whiskey. Two young people needlessly died because of a dispute over liquor. The two men responsible, Ed Glover and Bars Davis, had been drunk at the time and probably would not have carried out the crime had they been sober. Many suspected that A.H. Byars, too, might have been killed by members of the same whiskey ring. Many believed that Macon's citizens would have to take matters into their own hands if the city council and the police were unable or unwilling to wipe out the making and sale of bootleg whiskey.

The men leading this "call to arms" were the city's ministers and the editors of its two newspapers, the Macon *Telegraph* and the *Macon News*. Joining forces, they exposed from their pulpits and editorial columns how the flagrant violation of prohibition laws in the city bred a disrespect for law and order and led to murders like those of E.W. Wilson and Hilda Smith. Dr. William Russell Owen of the First Baptist Church blamed Macon's citizens, particularly those with wealth and social standing, for the wave of crime brought on by illicit whiskey. It was they who kept the snake that was the bootlegger alive. "Bootleggers are like a great writhing serpent," he claimed. With every purchase of whiskey, the "so-called good citizens" were keeping it "crawling and writhing on its way of lawlessness and death and desolation."[156]

Owen stated that men on the church rolls and in some of Macon's most respected civic organizations were buying and drinking bootleg whiskey. Such men, he said, were Judases who were betraying their community. They could, however, find redemption by supporting vigorous enforcement of the liquor laws. In doing so, they would be protecting the city's boys and girls. "Poor Hilda Smith," he concluded, "depended in vain on good citizenship to protect her!"[157]

Not to be outdone, Reverend J. Peacock of Vineville Methodist Church compared the effort to stop bootlegging to Rome's struggle to conquer the wicked city of Carthage. "Rome tried for 215 years to take and destroy the city of Carthage and the war against the liquor traffic extends over a hundred years." In a reference to the murders on Swift Creek Road, he maintained that if "city and county officials had taken drastic steps to wipe out this evil in the Macon community the cries in two homes in our midst would not have been." He asked that the righteous people of Macon "stand over these newly made graves and cry out 'we two [*sic*] will remember you and try to make it impossible for another like tragedy.'" Like Dr. Owen, he called on churches, civic clubs and the chamber of commerce to support a city- and countywide crusade against whiskey.[158]

Reverend Luther Harrell of the Cherokee Heights Methodist Church echoed the assertions of his fellow ministers. He exhorted the churchgoing people of Macon to take action. "I know of no institution or organization that can do more to check lawlessness than the church. The majority of the people of our country and section are either members of some church or favorably inclined to it." Christians had a responsibility, he said, to "create such a sentiment that will cause an enforcement of our laws."[159]

Adopting the slogan "Buyers and sellers of bootleg whiskey are undesirable citizens of Macon. Get out and stay out," ministers continued to hold rallies against liquor trafficking during the investigation into the Swift Creek Road murders. On July 25, three ministers—Dr. Walter Anthony, Reverend B.F. Foster and Dr. Owen—planned a mass meeting of three Macon church congregations at Mulberry Street Methodist Church. Their goal was to condemn "booze and the bootlegger."[160]

But before the rally, police chief Ben Watkins asked Dr. Owen to accompany him and his officers on several raids on blind tigers in the city. He wanted the minister to see how difficult it was to get the evidence the city needed to arrest, let alone convict, bootleggers.[161]

As Dr. Owen learned during the raids, bartenders kept their liquor in a pitcher or a coffeepot underneath the bar adjacent to a tub of creolin, vinegar or some other chemical. When a lookout alerted the bartender that police officers were approaching, he knocked the liquor into the tub. The practice made it impossible to smell or taste the alcohol, and without the alcohol, officers could not make an arrest.[162]

Despite the difficulty in obtaining the evidence needed to arrest and convict bootleggers, since January 1, 1926, the police department had been conducting daily raids. According to Chief Watkins, known blind tigers, many of them located along Broadway and in the Tybee District, were raided as many as two to six times every twenty-four hours. There were usually few arrests, and despite the frequency of the raids, operators and distributors kept the liquor flowing. "The minute we leave a place," said the chief, "the manager or proprietor telephones to his wholesaler or distributor to send him another gallon or half gallon." Using young boys as runners, distributors then quickly dispatched the liquor to the blind tiger by car. Officers were sent back to the establishments to make sure no more liquor was delivered there. But more often than not, the driver spotted the guard and drove on without leaving the whiskey. This did temporarily prevent the flow of liquor in one location, but there were so many joints in the city that the department didn't have enough officers to guard them.[163]

The arrest and conviction of operators and distributors was also slowed by the legal system. Every time officers raided an establishment, they had to get a warrant. Because they raided twenty to thirty joints a day, one man, said the chief, was kept busy twelve hours a day writing warrants. If by chance they were able to get enough evidence to go to court, bootleggers and their lawyers were highly skilled in negotiating light sentences and delaying trials. Of course, when they did go to trial, juries were not inclined to convict. Many, not surprisingly, patronized the blind tigers or purchased their liquor directly from the bootleggers. Some had even told the chief that he and his department were "overdoing it" and that they "should not be so hard on the bootlegger: just think of the people you know yourself who patronize them."[164]

The rally that the ministers organized for July 25 promised "war without quarter" and adopted a series of resolutions. Prohibition, they said, was the law of the land and must be enforced. They asserted their intention to vote only for candidates who were dry and called on officials to "guarantee that all their deputies and helpers be personally dry." They recommended that more officers be hired to watch known blind tigers, and believing that fines were no deterrence to the bootlegger, they demanded that the courts sentence all violators of prohibition laws to jail or the chain gang. Tempering their strident tone somewhat, they said that they believed there was "some good in the heart of every bootlegger and appealed to his best manhood and to his sense of citizenship, that he quit the illegal traffic and join with us in our campaign for a better America."[165]

To spread their message, they would enlist the help of the print media. Advertising agencies would be hired to produce posters that would be displayed throughout the city. But their crusade desperately needed the support of the city's newspapers. The ministers implored them to condemn whiskey, bootleggers and blind tigers and not to print editorials or cartoons that made light of prohibition laws.

The editors of both the *Macon News* and the Macon *Telegraph* took up the fight. In a number of editorial columns, they endorsed the ministers' resolutions and pledged to expose the lawlessness that bootlegging fostered in the city. The *Macon News* was the most enthusiastic in its support. "The preachers were right," read one editorial. "Whiskey and crime go hand in hand; they are the twin monsters of the darkness with whiskey the leader in many instances." The column said bootleggers were "the lowest of the low" and that they "could make no claim to being good citizens, civic leaders, or indifferent residents."[166]

In another editorial, titled "Liquor and Murder," the paper commended the preachers for their crusade to clean up the city and for calling attention to the role that bootlegging played in the deaths of E.W. and Hilda. While the editors realized that many of Macon's high and mighty "liked their liquor," these same citizens, they said, were culpable in promoting the crime that was defaming the city. Macon, they said, was "one of the fairest flowers of the South; its name cannot be insulted by booze guzzlers and booze vendors. It is high time that this terrible traffic be stopped."[167]

The *Macon News* became an unabashed defender of the most militant of the crusade's preachers: Reverend A.C. Baker of the Tabernacle Baptist Church. Baker, for example, said in a sermon he titled "The Truth About the Whisky Traffic in Bibb County" that the sheriff's office and the police were complicit in protecting bootleggers in certain sections of the city and county. "Our bootleggers do a great business in a certain alley. People go in and out of there for that purpose at all hours of the day and night. Do you hear of any raids in this protected part of our city?" These protected vendors of whiskey were contributing to widespread drunkenness and destroying families. Ladies in the city, he said, called him almost daily about the prevalence of whiskey drinking in their neighborhoods. Their husbands, he said, were good friends with the wholesalers and retailers of whiskey and were coming home drunk most every night.[168]

Baker blamed the mayor and city council. They, he believed, had instructed law enforcement to go after not the wealthy, organized bootleggers but the smaller retailers. Why? Although he never said it flat-out, he suggested that they were accepting bribes or feared that bootleggers' customers would turn against them at the ballot box. Some officers and judges, he mused, were perhaps just wet in their sentiments and were inclined to not enforce the law or hand down heavy sentences. Macon's citizens would have to recognize their role in creating the deplorable conditions in the city. "Our people have failed to do their duty," he said. Referring to E.W. and Hilda, he said, "Every person that voted for the present administration had a hand in the double murder that shocked our people recently."[169]

Outraged by the role that bootleg whiskey played in the killing of Hilda Smith and E.W. Wilson, Reverend A.C. Baker of the Tabernacle Baptist Church blamed city and county officials for their failure to stop the illegal traffic in liquor. *Courtesy of the Macon* Telegraph.

Baker's accusations aroused the ire of city officials as well as much of the public. Nevertheless, he retained wide support, and in a followup to his previous sermon, he renewed his attack on the mayor, the city council, the police and the sheriff. Before a large congregation at his church, he claimed, as he had before, that he had signed affidavits about the complicity of city officials in the liquor trade.[170]

Baker's relentless attacks led to the calling of a special grand jury. If he had evidence of impropriety on the part of the city and county's law enforcement officials, he must present it through the proper legal channels. Solicitor General Charles H. Garrett was instructed by the grand jury to issue a subpoena for the affidavits Baker claimed he had in his possession. If the documents were not placed in the jury's hands, Baker could be found guilty of contempt, or he could be indicted for libel.[171]

The city council avoided, for the most part, any discussion of the Baker matter. It thought that the chief and his detectives were doing their all to abate the liquor situation. "I believe the council realizes," said Mayor Wallace Miller, "that the police department is doing its duty and is very aggressive. It's easier to tell how the prohibition law be enforced than to enforce it."[172]

Like Dr. Owen, Reverend Baker was asked to see for himself the difficulties law enforcement faced in shutting down bootlegging operations in the city and county. "A city detective came to me this week and wanted me to go on a raid, saying 'I want to show you how impossible it is to catch them so you can tell the people.'" But Baker was having none of it; he believed that sympathetic "wet" police officers and sheriff's deputies notified liquor dealers in advance of raids. "They cannot put that thin stuff in my head; neither can they make a fool out of this preacher." He declined the invitation, believing that he and other ministers were being hoodwinked.[173]

After Baker turned over the affidavits, the grand jury made a thorough investigation into their authenticity and the veracity of the charges made against the sheriff's office. While it found that liquor was definitely being made, sold and drunk in the county, there was no evidence that the sheriff or his deputies were in league with the bootleggers. "Our investigations convince us," read the report, "that he is courageous and efficient in the administration of his office; that he meets any public emergency tactfully and fearlessly, and that in directing his subordinates in quest of those who violate the laws, he is always positive and aggressive, and sometimes even harsh."[174] They believed that Baker was motivated by good intentions, but "we deplore the ill-advised zeal which has impelled him to cast odious reflections on Bibb County, and some of its public officers." As for the accusations made by others, the jurors found them "groundless." They concluded that they "emanated from a small group of persons who very probably have a lively interest in the political adversities of Sheriff Hicks."[175]

In the years following 1926, the ministers' crusade to drive the whiskey ring out of the city and county lost its fervor. Although they preached against the evils of alcohol and the bootlegger, most ministers eventually reconciled themselves to the fact that the police and the sheriff's department were doing all they could to slow the liquor traffic. The double murder that spurred the campaign was not forgotten, but there seemed to be little evidence that bootlegging was causing a wave of violent crime in Middle Georgia. By the mid-1930s many of the same ministers who fought liquor would turn their attention to a vice they believed was as much of a threat to the public good as alcohol: gambling.

Chapter 10

THE FEVER

Macon's citizens liked to think of themselves as hardworking, churchgoing folk who avoided the vices that plagued other cities. But Macon, as many knew, had always had a cross section of people who enjoyed the excitement of card games, craps and lotteries or numbers rackets in various forms. By the early 1930s, the number of gambling houses had grown exponentially, many operating twenty-four hours a day throughout downtown, along Broadway and in the Tybee District. Macon's ministers were alarmed. It seemed the city was in the midst of a gambling fever that threatened to destroy its moral foundations.

Even society ladies, complained ministers, were being seduced by the gaming tables. While they did not play bridge or whist for money, it was not uncommon, for example, for hosts to offer prizes to the players who scored the most points. When reporters from the Macon *Telegraph* asked a number of the city's prominent women if this practice was the same as gambling, they scoffed at the idea. "I don't think it is wrong in playing bridge for a pretty prize," said Mrs. E.W. Gould. "It adds zest to the game and makes a pleasant afternoon for a group of players." Mrs. Fort E. Land echoed those sentiments: "A pretty prize adds to the party in the same manner that flowers would. I never objected to playing for a prize, but would not play for money."[176]

When asked their opinion, however, the city's ministers all seemed to agree that whether playing for a porcelain teacup or cash money, it was still gambling. Dr. W.F. Quillian, president of Wesleyan College and pastor of

Mulberry Street Methodist Church, said the "playing of every game for a prize has in it the element of chance. It is therefore a dangerous tendency to engage in such games for any stakes whatever." Dr. Charles H. Lee, pastor of St. Paul's Episcopal Church, saw particular harm in playing bridge for prizes. "People waste valuable time," he said, "become bridge fiends and lose their tempers."[177]

Worse yet, said some citizens, it was not becoming of a proper woman and mother. "A man gambling is an abominable weakness; with a woman it's an intolerable and inexcusable wrong," wrote Eli Grac in a letter to the Macon *Telegraph*. "Societyhood is a poor substitute for womanhood, and real mothers cannot be members of society that actually gamble."[178]

At the urging of ministers and concerned citizens, the mayor and the city council initiated an anti-gambling campaign. Beginning in 1933, Mayor G. Glen Toole ordered the police department to shut down lotteries and slot machines that operated in retail stores, soft drink shops and other businesses.[179]

One of the most popular games was the baseball lottery. Players received cash prizes if they'd purchased a ticket with the name of the teams that had scored the highest number of runs. While the prices and winnings varied, most tended to purchase a twenty-five-cent cent ticket that paid nine dollars to the winner. Every baseball season, claimed the mayor, Macon's citizens spent thousands of dollars on the game, with few ever seeing any winnings.

But thousands of dollars also went into a variety of gambling machines. Throughout the city, there were establishments where gamblers could play what was known as the "derby," a type of slot machine that represented a horse race. The player put in a coin, selected a horse and pulled the crank. If the horse happened to win, he received money through a slot in the side. Depending on the amount put into the machine, the payoff could be sizeable.

"Bucket shops" were another common form of gambling in the city that the mayor wanted to shut down. These small "investment" firms had been around since the late nineteenth century and were responsible for bilking customers out of thousands of dollars. Preying on those who wanted to make quick money by speculating on stock prices, they would advise their customers to buy shares of a particular stock that the firm counted on dropping in price. The customer's money was placed or "bucketed" into the firm's account. When the stock dropped in price, as the firm expected, it reported a loss and pocketed the customer's money. Occasionally, the firm would guess wrong and have to pay up.[180]

As in the movement against blind tigers and bootleggers, it was the city's ministers who would lead the charge. Dr. Joseph P. Boone of the First Baptist Church was greatly concerned about the presence of pinball machines and other devices in the city's stores. Such devices, he said, "appeal to the gambling spirit, particularly among children and young people." He called on the city's "best citizens" to stop gambling in Macon.[181]

By 1934, many of Macon's citizens recognized that gambling was all too common in the city and believed it should be ended. According to Solicitor General Charles H. Garrett, there was a "rising tide of indignation" among a majority of Macon's citizens regarding the open gambling that was taking place in downtown businesses. He urged citizens to help him collect direct evidence so he could present it to the grand jury.[182]

In November 1934, Dr. Baker, chairman of the minister's campaign against gambling, stated that he and the city's pastors were not satisfied with either the public or law enforcement's efforts to destroy the slot machines and lotteries that were operating in the city and county. In support of the campaign, ministers attacked gambling in all its forms in their Sunday sermons and expressed their frustration with law enforcement. "It was the duty of city and county officials to protect the public and enforce the law," said Dr. Mackay of the First Presbyterian Church. "Ministers are not policemen," he proclaimed, "but their duty is to uncover evil and to denounce sin." Reverend Small of the First Christian Church, president of the Macon Ministerial Association, said that "an aroused public conscience demands action" and that officers of the law must gather the necessary evidence and vigorously prosecute the offenders.[183]

By early January 1935, Dr. Baker and the city's ministers had grown impatient and amplified their call for action. Assembling in the YMCA auditorium, they demanded protection for "Macon's civic righteousness" and expressed their alarm at the staggering growth of gambling and other vices in the city. There was too much at stake, and they would not be silent. Pinball machines and other devices for amusement were corrupting the city's youth. "We must give our boys a chance," he declared. "Even public school boys are crowding gambling devices daily....Our committee has made a thorough investigation of local conditions and we find that so-called game devices are being used for gambling in every instance."[184]

One solution, said a number of ministers, was to get into politics and get more true Christians registered to vote. Local officials would act, said Dr. C.C. Yarborough, a dentist and deacon of Tabernacle Baptist, "when they are in fear of losing their jobs." They would have to form a large

Men, women and children in Macon played the many slot machines that were discreetly hidden in many businesses during the 1930s and '40s. *Courtesy of the Time Detective Gallery.*

organization, most agreed, that would bring political pressure to bear on the mayor and city council.[185]

Dr. Scarborough, like the ministers, believed that Macon's officials were under the spell of dark forces. Later, in December 1935, when he appeared before the judge in recorder's court to answer to a traffic ticket, he expressed his resentment that the police were stepping up their enforcement of traffic laws while doing nothing about widespread vice in the city. "The underworld has got this town by the tail," he proclaimed, and "everybody knows how many places whisky is sold openly and without fear of the law and there is gambling on every hand."[186]

Leaders of the anti-gambling campaign saw no evidence that gambling and other vices had abated in 1936. In fact, they believed the situation had gotten worse. In their sermons on May 17, Dr. Baker, Reverend James R. Webb of Cherokee Heights Baptist Church and Reverend Silas Johnson, pastor of Vineville Baptist Church, once again called on the city to go after the gambling houses.[187]

Not surprisingly, Dr. Baker was the most forceful in his remarks. Crime and all forms of vice, he stated, had the upper hand in Macon. "Gambling of practically every type is going on in the open; men, women, boys, and girls are all gambling. Thousands of dollars are being spent daily." He assured his congregation that he was going to do all he could to clean up the city and make it a decent place to live.[188]

Dr. Baker then gave the mayor and city council an ultimatum. If they did not put a halt to the deplorable conditions, he was going to call a mass meeting for men only at his church. He planned for two thousand men and boys to hear testimonials from twenty-five men who had not only purchased whiskey throughout the city but had also gambled on every device in the Middle Georgia underworld.[189]

Dr. Baker declared that it was high time for Christians to "get out in the open and fight" and that he was ready to take personal command of cleaning up the city if officials did not act immediately. But even if they did take action, he was "going to be the one to say when it's clean enough." Many in his congregation, he said, probably regretted that he had been so vocal in his criticisms of city officials. But any member who objected to his campaign could remove their membership. "If you think I'm the man to keep his mouth shut, you're wrong," he proclaimed.[190]

Facing pressure from Dr. Baker and fellow ministers, the Macon city police stepped up their raids on gambling houses in the city. During the state Democratic convention that was held in Macon in October 1936, dice games, slot machines and poker games were broken up. But it was not an easy task. Owners of gambling houses were ingenious in their efforts to elude the police. In order to avoid detection, they hid their operations in remote corners of the city. And by using peepholes in doors, they were able to scrutinize their customers. As a result, the city's police found it close to impossible to get enough evidence to charge anyone when they raided these establishments.

City officials, however, had made it hot for those who dared to run slot machines, poker games and roulette wheels in their businesses. Ministers applauded these efforts, but by the end of the decade, they saw evidence that a new form of the gambling fever had seized the city.

The "Bug," as it was known, was a lottery in which a player selected three sequential numbers that he hoped would match the number of sales for that day on the stock and bond market. Operated by the Old Line Company and its subsidiaries, this gambling syndicate had offices throughout the country. In cities like Macon, players purchased their tickets either at retail stores or from young boys called "runners." Players could buy a ticket for as little as a penny or as much as ten dollars. With a payoff of 500 to 1, a player could reap substantial winnings if his number hit. But a bettor only had a 1 in 999 chance of winning. At those odds, the company was able to take in an average of $1 million a year in the late 1930s.[191]

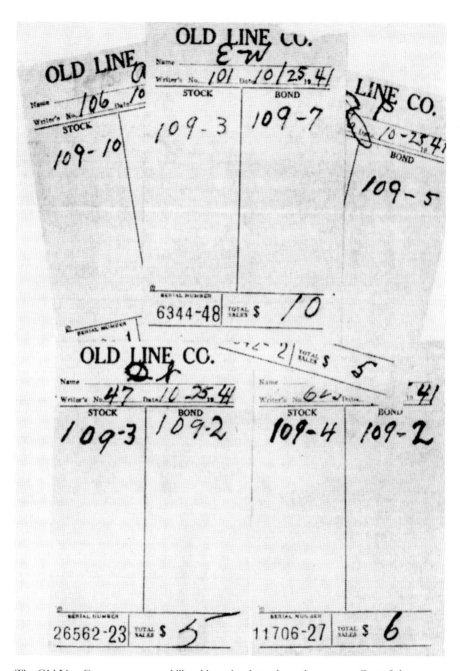

The Old Line Company operated illegal lotteries throughout the country. One of the most popular in Macon was the "Bug." Runners, as they were called, sold tickets like the one pictured here on the downtown streets and in the Tybee District. *Courtesy of the* Macon News.

To give the syndicate the look of legitimacy, the company issued tickets on printed forms that bore the company's name. Legend had it that its subsidiaries were required to maintain solid bank balances and that during hard times, they had helped smaller offices pay off rather than risk damage to the company's reputation and hurting the game. "Like Old Man River," said the *Macon News* in an expose about the company, "the racket keeps rolling along—undisturbed, unmolested, and sweeping a great flow of good hard cash into the pockets of the racketeers."[192]

By 1941, the Bug was, as reported by the *Macon News*, the city's "biggest and most solidly established racket." Even though it had no license, it ran without any interference from law officers and had players from all walks of life: "It operates as openly as any legitimate business, employing scores of runners, pick-up men and clerks and extending its grasping fingers alike into Negro shacks and prosperous business offices." It was estimated that the Bug took $3,000 per day from the city's citizens.[193]

Bug players, according to interviews conducted by the *Macon News*, said they found the game exhilarating and saw no harm in it. Although most had never scored big winnings or even won, they played daily. But a number had been lucky enough to pick numbers that hit and hoped that one day they would win big. All confirmed that the company quickly paid off.

Many Bug players were superstitious and relied on dreams and other signs for the numbers they played. A house number, a sales ticket from a restaurant, a scrap of paper found on the street or a number in a newspaper might have the combination that was going to hit big for that day. When the *Macon News* investigated the Bug racket in the city, for example, it printed a photograph of a losing ticket with the number 109. Believing this to be some sort of mysterious sign, hundreds of people bet their money on 109 the following day. It didn't hit, of course, but sales for that number, said Bug operators, broke all records.[194]

By the fall of 1941, the mayor and city council were receiving weekly complaints from ministers, business leaders, civic groups and the editors of the *Macon News* about the effrontery with which the Bug operated in the city. It not only brought financial strain on families but also robbed merchants of thousands of dollars in valuable trade. But without a specific ordinance or state law, city officials could not take action. After much pressure, the mayor and council passed an ordinance aimed specifically at the Bug that forbade the operation of a lottery within the city. Soon after, it authorized the police department to begin a campaign to close all Bug offices and to confiscate books of lottery tickets. The campaign, which was spurred by the

Macon News's reporting, resulted in the city's Bug offices closing before they could actually be raided. "The racketeers," said the *News*, "had fled before publicity and police like rats before an army of stray cats."[195]

But apparently, they hadn't gone far. By early December, there were increasing reports of lottery tickets being sold in eating houses in the railroad yards and in small businesses in the Tybee District. Determined to keep the Bug suppressed, the mayor and city council ordered the police to investigate these reports. Once again, Bug offices, now operating in less visible sections of the city, closed before they could be raided. The Bug, it appeared, was all but finished in Macon.[196]

Nevertheless, while the various lotteries and other forms of gambling had been curtailed or put out of business, there still remained the question of what to do about the large number of prostitutes who worked the boardinghouses, hotels and streets throughout the city since the closing of Tybee. City officials, the police department, businessmen and ministers had differing opinions. Many believed that the best way to contain the spread of prostitution and venereal disease was to reopen the red-light district. Not surprisingly, there would be an equal number who were vehemently opposed. As a result, the battle that the city experienced over prostitution before 1917 would be rejoined during the years leading up to World War II.

Chapter 11

PUT 'EM WHERE THEY BELONG

*S*ince coming to the police department, Zula Hamilton McCord, Macon's only policewoman for over twenty-six years, had taken on the responsibility of looking after the women who made their living as prostitutes in the city's brothels and streets. These women, she believed, had come to their vocation not from seduction but for a variety of other reasons. Most had chosen their path and were not interested in reforming. By the mid-1930s, McCord had decided that the best way to protect them and the rest of the city from disease and the other harmful effects of the trade was to reestablish the red-light district. Most of the city's ministers as well as many officials, however, refused to support her campaign for a regulated district. Nevertheless, there would be civic organizations, physicians and even a few religious leaders who found McCord's argument convincing and rallied to her side.

Born in Texas in 1890, Zula Hamilton moved with her family to Cordele, where she attended the public schools. At seventeen, she married W.E. McCord and moved to Macon. The couple soon started a family and by the late 1920s had four daughters. Although a devoted mother and church worker, Zula believed there was much more she could do to improve life for the city's young people.[197]

Based on reports coming from the police and the courts, there was a crisis. "The conditions that exist in this city are unbelievable," said Judge Hugh Evans of the Bibb County juvenile court.

We have mothers in this town who are using their daughters freely for commercial purposes. An investigation of a section of the city disclosed to juvenile court officers last week that 16 Macon children under 15 years of age were living in houses of prostitution. The only way we can remedy this situation is to provide adequate housing facilities for these girls whose parents are not fit to take care of them.[198]

Mrs. W.E. McCord, later known as "Ma" to her fellow officers, was Macon's first and only policewoman for twenty-six years. During the 1930s, she asked city officials to reestablish the red-light district. *Courtesy of the* Macon News.

But building dormitories, he admitted, would not prevent young girls from being drawn to prostitution as long as the city turned a blind eye to the brothels. According to the judge, "The city knows the houses of prostitution are here, and they should be cleaned out, if you have to take a torch to them."[199]

Faced with an unprecedented rise in sex trafficking and juvenile delinquency, the city council decided in 1928 to appoint Zula and Mrs. George L. Wasner as special officers to the police department. Their assignment would be to help young women and children who had either fallen into prostitution or had been abandoned.

Although promised the standard policeman's pay of $125 per month, they ended up going to work for $50 per month. The two worked feverishly their first few months on the job to assist those in need. But the council provided no funding, and the two spent most of their pay buying food and clothing for unfortunate women and children. The officers asked the mayor and council to fulfill their promise, but they refused.[200]

In response, the two tendered their resignations and then provided the council with a detailed report on the many cases they had handled. Those who read the report were impressed with their selfless commitment to wayward girls:

Our first work was with three young girls who were brought to police headquarters....The case was turned over to us, and after a thorough investigation we found that these girls had gone very far in sin. Not having a place that we could place them we kept them at the city hall until some disposition could be made of them, and after several days of trying we located relatives of two of the girls, not the mother or father—for they were dead. The sister of one refused to take her, saying to us in a letter, "She has brought disgrace on our family and we can't take her back." Even this did not dishearten us, for we knew that somewhere, someone was willing to help the girl who wanted to help herself.[201]

Eventually, they were proven right. The girl whose family rejected her was placed in "one of Macon's best Christian homes." The other two girls were also fortunate. One was sent to Miami to live with her stepmother, while the other was placed with a respected family in Atlanta.[202]

Despite her unfair treatment by the mayor and council, McCord knew that helping young women and children was her calling. In 1930, she accepted a position as a deputy probation officer under the direction of the Bibb County juvenile court. But prostitution was so rampant in Macon that the city asked her to return to the police force as a special officer for women's and girls' affairs. This time, she would receive equal pay. She served in this capacity until her retirement in 1954.[203]

Matronly and standing only five feet tall, Officer McCord proved to be both a tireless and intrepid defender of the ladies and young girls who worked the brothels in the city as well as families who had little or no food during the depression years. She passed judgment on no one and was always willing to help anyone in need. She later explained that she "was always interested in the underdog, don't you know?"[204]

Over the course of her career, she had seen it all. Between 1930 and the end of the war, Macon was a wide open town, and the police had their work cut out for them. Many didn't think women would make good officers. But "Ma," as she came to be known, proved them wrong. Although she never carried a gun, she broke up fights, corralled drunks and raided brothels and gambling houses. One arrest she always found amusing. "I was riding on Broadway one day and saw two men fighting with big sticks," she recalled. "I got out of my car, walked over to them and asked, 'Don't you know someone is going to get hurt?'" Unsure of just who this diminutive woman was, they stopped fighting. Motioning to the backseat, she told them to get in the car. The men submissively got into the car. They were quite surprised when they arrived at the police department.[205]

Ma, however, had many heartbreaking experiences that stuck with her to her final days. In an interview with the Macon *Telegraph* in 1949, she recounted the story of a girl she called Elsie. "She was a young girl, and I thought I had straightened her out four different times, but each time, she would drift back to her old life, although she hated it." Like so many girls during the Depression years, Elsie found jobs hard to come by, and she needed money.[206]

Ma remained hopeful that Elsie might turn from prostitution, but one night, a detective called her from a downtown hotel. He had something he wanted to show her:

> *I went and they were just cutting Elsie down from where she had hanged herself from the room fan fixture. She had tied the cord of her bathrobe around the fixture, fastened it around her neck while she stood on the foot of the bed and jumped off. I think she must have changed her mind when she started to strangle, because one hand was wedged between her neck and the cord in a futile effort to loosen it.*[207]

Ma thought she had failed Elsie and considered resigning.

But for every Elsie, there was a young girl she saved. Not long after taking the job, she was called to investigate a girl who was seen going into an abandoned warehouse behind the railroad tracks on Eighth Street. After arriving, she entered the dark, damp building and gingerly headed down the basement stairs. She could see that there was a young girl seated on a box against the back wall. "Don't come near me," she yelled. But Ma moved closer and said, "I'm your friend." The girl was not to be consoled. "You're not my friend," she cried. "I haven't a friend in the world." Ma could see that the girl had a bottle of what she suspected to be poison. She had come to this forbidding place to end her life.[208]

Ma was eventually able to gain the girl's trust. She learned that her name was Elaine and that she had been working in one of the more upscale brothels in town. But once the madam discovered that she had contracted a venereal disease, she was turned out.[209]

Ma got Elaine to a doctor for treatment and found her a home with a good woman. Eventually, Elaine was offered a job as a housekeeper for a man who had no children and had lost his wife. He became quite taken with her, despite her background. The two married and lived comfortably in the country. But a year later, Elaine died from complications of pregnancy. Although her story was in many ways tragic, she at least passed from the earth knowing she was loved.[210]

Unlike many of the crusaders against vice in Macon, Ma took a kindhearted but practical approach to the problem of prostitution. Her experience had left her with little use for those who thought vigorous enforcement of the law would cure society of the "social evil." She knew better and would find herself doing battle with the sanctimonious idealists of the city.

By the mid-1930s, she had come to believe that a segregated district was the best way to not only contain venereal disease but also protect the young women who chose prostitution as their vocation. Ma had spent many years working in the district and was well acquainted with the women who plied their trade in Tybee. They, as she soon came to realize, were not innocent victims of "white slavery" or children of abusive homes. Just how they came to embrace the "sporting life" was far more complicated, but based on her experience, they all shared much in common:

> *I regard a prostitute as a product of social degeneration. After working with hundreds of them I find they have certain outstanding psychological traits. They fear planned living; they have complete apathy; they have repugnance to family life and living with the same man, and they have a love of riotous living and pleasures of all sorts.....Not all of their good instincts are dead. The prostitute may love her keeper with an idolatrous passion, and one is sometimes surprised by her strong maternal feelings. She is generous to a fault—and almost always destitute.*[211]

In Macon, in particular, she found that "about 45 percent came from small towns and farms within 100 miles of Macon. Eight percent had been employed in mills and in other industrial plants. The origin of the other 47 per cent is unknown." More than likely, they came from the "poor working classes."[212]

Conditions in the city were out of control, she maintained in a 1935 Macon *Telegraph* and *Macon News* interview. "There are in Macon between 40 and 50 houses generally regarded as houses of prostitution here and in each house there may be found from one to 12 girls and young women," she observed. Together with the open houses, there was also, she said, an extensive network of clandestine prostitution.[213]

Attempting to end prostitution in Macon was futile. "When we raid a place and happen to get evidence that justifies a court trial, it is usually only temporary relief. The inmates scatter to other sections of town and conditions become worse." She believed "a segregated district would certainly solve that phase of the question."[214]

Ma asked the city council and the police commission to consider establishing a segregated red-light district that "would be under police and medical supervision." She maintained that such a district "would be a great step forward in the control of vice." The mayor and council, however, feared that there would be strong resistance from local ministers and were reluctant to act.[215]

But Ma was adamant and took her case to a number of women's organizations. After listening to her argument for a segregated district, the Auxiliary to the Joseph N. Neal Jr. Unit 3 of the American Legion presented a resolution to the Committee on Police to establish a "restricted district for women of ill repute." They noted that Macon had a red-light district before the First World War and argued that "it would be far better for the people of Macon if these women were placed in restricted districts with adequate policing and medical attention, so that this vice might be regulated to the betterment of the city's health and social conditions." The committee took the petition on advisement and promised to report to the council after they had gathered information from all interested parties.[216]

Just as the committee suspected, a number of ministers denounced the proposal from the pulpit. Dr. J.A. Harmon of the Centenary Methodist Church said, "Such a position would be a disgrace in this enlightened age and a backward step that would make every citizen who stands for purity and decency blush with shame."[217]

The editors of the Macon *Telegraph* echoed Dr. Harmon's objections. "A red-light district is a place for fallen women and falling men who have lost all self-respect and sense of shame, who are willing to acknowledge to the world that they are hopeless, and have chosen the degraded, outlawed, vicious ruination of body and soul." Such a district, they claimed, would be "a miasma of degradation" that would envelop "the city like a malarial scourge, as an indictment and conviction of a community that recognizes and by recognition approves of such an enterprise."[218]

But surprisingly, there were those in the religious community who fully supported a segregated district. Evangelist J. Montague Power, in a letter to the Macon *Telegraph*, recalled the years before World War I when the Tybee District was operating freely. During those days, he said, "no woman, recognized as a harlot, was permitted to inhabit the realms of decency." But with the closing of the segregated district, "we find every hotel, boarding house, also apartment house infected with these putrid, painted harlots." Power stated that he was "an ardent supporter of a segregated district, where these denizens of the underworld can cavort and apply their rotten trade." He expressed "profound admiration for the splendid police woman here, who had the courage to advocate the re-establishment of the Red-Light District." It was best to "put 'em where they belong, and keep 'em there."[219]

The members of the police committee and the council watched through the spring and summer as the debate intensified and then fizzled. A search of the minutes for the remaining months of 1935 and the forthcoming year turns up no mention of the issue. Either the police committee never reported back to the council, or if it did, it didn't want its findings included in the minutes.

By 1937, the number of syphilis cases had spiked, and the city had to do something. The police department, decided the council, would have to declare war on the city's lewd houses. In a series of raids beginning in May, Ma and department detectives managed to close a number of houses and arrest the occupants.[220]

But this was just a start. Conditions in the houses were "positively shocking," said Ma. "We called in public health authorities, and they have found many girls and men who have contracted these dreadful diseases. As long as conditions like these are permitted to continue we will never be able to reduce the number of syphilis victims here." The only remedy, she said, was to require all diseased women and men who resided in houses of ill repute to get treatment or go to jail.[221]

Despite the fact that the treatment only cost twenty-five cents, some women of the underworld fled the city. "Several of these women known to us have left town in the last day or two," said Ma. "We went to a house on Oak Street Tuesday and notified three girls there that they would be examined. When we went back with the public health nurse yesterday we found the doors locked and the house vacant."[222] Just why they left is uncertain. They may have thought that they would never work in Macon again if word got out that they had tested positive. Of course, they may also have been suspicious or mistrustful of the treatment.[223]

There were some women who outright refused treatment. All such women, as Ma promised, were sent to the city jail or the county work farm for women. Others who failed to comply could avoid jail if they left the city. "Whenever such characters refuse treatment we will make every effort to run them out of the city," she remarked.[224]

The raids continued throughout the summer and fall with some degree of success. By November, Ma reported that the number of infections had gone down. But there still was a serious problem. Lab results of the women who were tested indicated that possibly one out of three prostitutes in the city had either syphilis or gonorrhea or both. Mrs. McCord pledged to continue the campaign "until every inmate of the 44 lewd houses in Macon has undergone tests." She also made it clear that the department would not back away from its policy of "get treated or go to jail."[225]

Contributing to the problem was that the raids had made it difficult for the inmates to earn enough money to pay the small fee to get treated for syphilis or gonorrhea. "Several of the women," said Ma, "have told me they were absolutely unable to pay the quarter required before they can begin treatment at the clinic." Many could no longer afford groceries. "Why I know for a fact," she commented, "that the trade at some of these houses has dropped off so much since the raids began, some of the inmates are having real trouble in buying meat and bread."[226]

While the raids had definitely slowed the sex trade, the high infection rate still remained. Ma explained that "in one house we raided recently there were five inmates. Four of them had syphilis. In another house there were four girls, all diseased. In three other houses raided, 12 girls were found to be diseased, and the tests of only nine were negative." These women desperately needed treatment, she said, if the city was going to stamp out venereal disease.[227]

But the answer, she still believed, lay not with more raids but with the reestablishment of a segregated vice district. She explained why in an interview with the Macon *Telegraph*:

> *The only solution, so far as I see it, is a regulated district, where we can keep constant watch on the women, and medical supervision over them. It's hard to have to admit you can't stamp out something like that—but you can't. It's been going on since the beginning of the world, and it'll continue to go on until the end.*[228]

Dr. C.L. Ridley, Macon hospital superintendent, agreed. "The practice of these women has been going on since the beginning of history, and it will be going on when we die. The red-light district, I believe, is the only answer to the problem."[229]

Realizing that the time had come to give McCord's suggestion serious consideration, the Macon *Telegraph* did an about-face from its position in 1935. It "appears logical that prostitution, segregated and medically supervised, would be less dangerous from a disease standpoint than prostitution scattered throughout a city without any more supervision than an occasional police raid when neighbors complain." The paper noted that Officer McCord's proposal had "met belligerent opposition from many well-meaning persons," including the *Telegraph*. These citizens were repulsed by any "official recognition that vice exists in Macon." "That sort of reaction," the editors admitted, "is not what should govern so serious a problem. It should be decided on a sensible basis from the standpoint of public health."[230]

By 1938, the city council appears to have given tacit approval to an "unofficial red-light district" situated along Broadway, Oak, Third, Plum and Ocmulgee. It was here, near the old Tybee District, that madams were generally free to operate their houses without police interference. The only requirement was that their inmates submit to regular physical examinations and that they take treatment if they tested positive for venereal disease. The hospital clinic waved the fee for those who couldn't pay.[231]

Prostitutes in the restricted area cooperated, and as a result, there was a decrease in venereal infections. Tests conducted in January 1938, stated Ma, "resulted in practically 100 negative reports." While the news regarding gonorrhea was less encouraging, there was still a slight decrease in positive tests. "When we have syphilis under control completely," she pledged, "we are going to devote more attention to the control of gonorrhea." It appeared the city was making progress against the spread of social disease.[232]

Chapter 12

DR. APPLEWHITE'S WAR

As war with Japan and Germany became imminent in the fall of 1941, young men all over the country entered the military. And with Camp Wheeler located only a few miles from the city, Macon would soon be home to thousands of soldiers. The city's public health official, Dr. J.L. Applewhite, feared the worst. Macon's red-light district had been operating undisturbed since 1939. If it wasn't closed, both the city and the camp's venereal disease rate were certain to climb.

Many found the district's presence a black spot on the city's image and called out government officials for not shuttering the houses. In an editorial titled "Who's Afraid of the Big Bad Law," the *Macon News* made light of the police's efforts at law enforcement.

> *Every conceivable kind of gambling currently flourishes under our very noses. Prostitutes brazenly solicit on our streets. A whole section of town is publicly recognized as the red-light district. And a plethora of tourist camps do a landslide business as houses of assignation where any foul-minded male can take one of the multitude of willing wenches not yet old or experienced enough to join the ranks of the professionals.*[233]

The piece ended with: "Law and Order! It is to Laugh."[234]

In another editorial, the *Macon News* said that the red-light district was an embarrassment to the city. "For us to tolerate a red light district is a mark of barbarism.…We point with pride to the cultural aspects of our city. We brag of intellectual stimuli found here.…We speak of Macon as a city of churches and universities and libraries....And yet we tolerate an open prostitution center."[235]

Unlike many critics of the red-light district, Dr. Applewhite was no crusading idealist. On the contrary, the Vanderbilt-and Harvard-trained physician's concern was that the district posed a serious threat to the health of the city and Camp Wheeler. But many of Macon's citizens feared that if the district was closed, prostitutes would scatter into the city.

Dr. Applewhite's hands, however, were tied; the United States Public Health Service wanted the district closed. Soon after, military police from Camp Wheeler and officers from Macon's police department entered the district and began shutting down the houses.

Dr. J.L. Applewhite, Macon's public health official, worked to contain the spread of venereal disease in the city and Camp Wheeler in the months leading up to World War II. Unlike Ma McCord, Dr. Applewhite refused to support the re-creation of the red-light district. *Courtesy of the Macon* Telegraph.

What happened next convinced observers that the vice problem would soon be far worse than before. One officer who oversaw the closings said the girls "scattered like a covey of quail" in taxicabs. Ma McCord commented that while she was closing one house, the inmates ordered rides to some of the city's hotels. "Obviously, many of the women forced out by the closing of the houses will scatter to cheap hotels and residences," she remarked. According to the Macon *Telegraph*, one madam said she had no intention of discontinuing her business:

> *One operator of an Oak Street house last night told a Telegraph reporter that she planned to construct an ornate house in the fashionable suburbs of Macon, outside the city limits. She said she plans to continue operations there in the residence, which will include among other elaborate fixtures, a neon sign.*[236]

It was going to be business as usual, only in a new and grander location.

Macon's citizens believed there was genuine cause for concern. The editors of the *Macon News*, for example, argued that if the United States Public Health Service wanted the district closed, it should be closed, but the Public Health Service must "insure that prostitutes are run out of town...and not out into town." In earlier years, said the paper, efforts to stamp out the red-light district had resulted in prostitutes scattering into hotels, apartments and residences in every part of the city. While it did not want to see the return of a segregated district, scarlet women "scattered through the city, in nice neighborhoods next door to decent, respectable people" would be disgraceful.[237]

T.M. Brundage, in a letter to the Macon *Telegraph*, explained that the executive officer of Camp Wheeler, Colonel A.R. Emery, believed that without a red-light district, the city "will be dirtier than ever." Colonel Emery had sparred with Dr. Applewhite over the rate of syphilis infections at the camp throughout October and November 1941 and believed that closing the district would scatter prostitutes "so badly that any supervision and health inspection is impossible." As Brundage concluded, the best way to contain venereal disease was to "have a supervised and medically examined 'district' and make everyone visit that station before leaving."[238]

Quite a few people objected to the government's decision. Businessmen, for example, complained that they stood to lose lots of money if the district was not reopened. In a meeting with Mayor Charles L. Bowden, a lawyer representing the owners of the houses in the district asked that the city "establish a red light district properly policed and with adequate medical examination provided." The city's merchants, as well, would be affected. They told the mayor and council that they would lose considerable money on goods that prostitutes had bought on installment plans.[239]

Two of the city's leading urologists believed that Dr. Applewhite and the Public Health Service were making a mistake. It was impractical to think that prostitution could be stopped. A controlled and regulated red-light district, they said, was preferable to one driven underground, where it would be impossible to keep the spread of disease in check. "Both insisted," reported the Macon *Telegraph*, "on periodic medical examination of the inmates of the district and that each person so examined be given a certificate which she be required to show."[240]

Dr. Applewhite disagreed. Camp Wheeler, he maintained, had more cases of venereal disease than any other base in Georgia. He was certain that the protected vice district was to blame and would not listen to the appeals of either the city's businessmen or other medical professionals. The city, with the help of the federal government, would have to do everything within its power to stamp out the source of the problem. "Experience has shown," asserted the doctor, "that practically all prostitutes become infected with these diseases and in time spread them to other people, so that, in any program for the control of these diseases, attention must be directed to this problem."[241]

Some people, he discovered, were willing to go to unusual lengths to keep the district open. F.W. Groome, a man claiming to be an undercover army intelligence officer, stated to city officials that he was there to conduct an investigation into the venereal disease problem and to assist the police in rounding up the prostitutes who worked the streets of the downtown area. In an interview with the *Macon News*, he maintained that the houses he visited were clean and that the army believed the best way to prevent the spread of disease among its soldiers was to reopen the district.

> *Our investigation has shown that a great majority of venereal infection comes from street walkers and immoral juke joint girls and not from the supervised and organized houses. I have personally investigated every one of the houses in the red light district and have found them to be clean. The system of supervision and examination that existed before the recently instituted crusade was one of the best I have ever seen. Every practical army officer knows that such a district properly run, is the best solution to problem of venereal disease in the army.*[242]

He predicted that city officials would follow the advice of the army and reopen the district in a few days.

Dr. Applewhite was suspicious. "I cannot understand how an army officer can ask that the district be re-opened when operation of a house of prostitution is a violation of both state and federal laws," he declared. He added that if "the police permit such a flagrant violation of the law I will report the matter to the state health department and ask that they take action to support my campaign against vice."[243]

Dr. Applewhite's suspicions were soon confirmed. The army and the FBI investigated and learned that the "army officer" who had aided police in arresting streetwalkers was actually an imposter. His name was Groome, but his only connection to the military was his recent employment as a carpenter at Camp Wheeler. Groome said he loved the thrill of police work and meant no harm. After spending a short time in jail for impersonating an officer, he was given probation and released.[244]

The most bizarre attempt to reopen the district, however, was a plot to assassinate Dr. Applewhite. Soon after the district's closing, a madam of one of the houses phoned Ma McCord about a man from Miami who said he would kill the doctor for $1,000. He claimed that he was originally from Chicago and had been a soldier in the Capone gang.[245]

Ma quickly informed her fellow officers and devised a ruse to trap the man. She would pose as a madam and meet with the would-be assassin. As she was plain and with no well-defined features, she knew she would need a more provocative and exotic look if she was to be convincing. Peering into the bathroom mirror of her home at 378 Suwanee Avenue, she carefully applied the lipstick and rouge she had recently purchased from the drugstore to her cheeks and lips. Still not quite satisfied, she applied a bit of eyeliner and put on a set of sparkling earrings. The floral dress and fashionable hat she had chosen completed her outfit, giving her just the appearance she was after for the meeting at an Oak Street brothel in the old Tybee red-light district.[246]

Shortly after she arrived, a man knocked on the door. When he entered, the madam of the house introduced Ma as "Fritzi" and said she ran the house across the street. The man balked and said he was not comfortable speaking to two people at a time. Fritzi said, "$1,000.00 is a lot of money. I have it and she hasn't. If you really want to liquidate Dr. Applewhite, you'll have to deal with me." The man walked over to the door and turned the key in the lock. He then put it in his pocket. Ma feared he planned to kill her.[247]

The man apparently was convinced, however, that Ma could be trusted and explained his qualifications for carrying out the murder. Apart from his

To establish his credentials as a killer, Frank Novak said that he once worked in the Al Capone organization in Chicago. At the time he made the claim, Capone was suffering from dementia brought on by syphilis, the very disease that Dr. Applewhite was trying to combat in Macon. *Courtesy of the Library of Congress.*

experience in the Chicago underworld, he had shot a Miami policeman and served eleven years of a twenty-year sentence. Ma concluded that the man fully intended to kill Dr. Applewhite and asked him for the key. "I'll go across the street to my house and get you $500.00," she said. "You can have the other $500.00 when the job is done." He nodded and handed her the key.[248]

Still unsure if the man might harm her and the other madam, Ma coolly unlocked the door. Outside stood Detective M.J. Huguley, a bear of a man, holding a pistol. Ma turned to the would-be assassin and said, "Young man, you are under arrest."[249]

Policewoman Zula Hamilton McCord, Macon's first and only policewoman for twenty-six years, had pulled off the ruse beautifully and, perhaps, saved Dr. J.D. Applewhite's life. Thankfully, the Oak Street madam who arranged the meeting had wanted no part of Novak's scheme and agreed to help Zula trap him.

At Macon police headquarters, the man confessed that he was Frank Novak, a thirty-year-old bank robber and car thief. And, as he had claimed, he was indeed from Chicago. But if he had ever had ties to the Capone organization, this could not be confirmed. However, if Novak had had any connections to Capone, he would have been very familiar with how profitable prostitution was to Chicago's crime syndicate. It's possible, then, that he believed the madams of Macon's demimonde so feared that their livelihood was to be taken from them that they might easily pay $1,000 for the elimination of the one man they felt responsible.[250]

But removing Dr. Applewhite would not reopen the district. The army and the Public Health Service were going to make sure it stayed closed. Yet even if the doctor's assassination could have somehow brought back the old district, Ma knew the ladies who operated the houses were not killers. And as she had said in numerous interviews with the Macon *Telegraph* and the *Macon News*, the madams were good-hearted women who were always willing to help the less fortunate. Once more, they had much respect for Ma and for the public health officials who were trying to prevent the spread of disease. They would not countenance or support the killing of a man who was simply doing his job.

Whether or not Novak ever intended to go through with the plot is uncertain. Had the police not stepped in, he may have just taken the money and left town. As much as the chief of police and the solicitor general of the city court wanted to charge Novak with conspiracy to commit murder, he had violated no statute. "He has not conspired to murder, because the conspiracy was never completed," said the solicitor. "He has not attempted

Frank Novak (*far right*) told one of Tybee's madams that he would kill Dr. Applewhite for $1,000. Ma and Detective M.J. Hugely (*left*) discuss the case soon after Novak's arrest. *Courtesy of the Macon* Telegraph.

to commit murder, obviously, for he made no overt act to commit murder," he added. The only charge that they could bring against him might be vagrancy, but that wouldn't stick if he could produce a small amount of money and an address. Eventually, Novak was released and left the city.[251]

Dr. Applewhite's friends and supporters, however, feared for his safety and believed that he should get police protection. The doctor scoffed at the notion. "There's no reason to kill me, and if I were killed another health officer would take my place to continue the anti-vice drive, which was ordered by the U.S. Public Health Service," he said.[252]

By 1942, reported the National Advisory Police Committee on Social Protection, Macon, like most cities in the United States, had succeeded in doing away with its red-light district. According to the committee, the latest reports from the army and navy indicated a substantial reduction in venereal cases "and proved false the fears in some communities that red-light districts were necessary and served as a crime deterrent, particularly sex crimes." The committee's findings, believed Dr. Applewhite, vindicated his efforts.[253]

But the committee said that the nation would have to open up a second front against another deadly source of venereal infection. Streetwalkers and the call girls who worked the tourist camps, dance halls and juke joints, it found, were a serious threat to the health of the armed forces. With over fourteen thousand men at Camp Wheeler and a growing number of prostitutes on downtown streets and in bars and cheap motels, Macon was in for a challenge.

Chapter 13

STREETWALKERS AND
JUKE JOINT SNIPERS

While Dr. Applewhite had officially closed the red-light district, prostitution and venereal infection still remained a problem. Soldiers at Camp Wheeler and the Army Air Corp Depot in Warner Robins who visited Macon could find assignations with the many streetwalkers who solicited business along the city's downtown streets. And in the juke joints and tourist camps both inside and outside the city, there were plenty of opportunities to hook up with working girls. Macon was fast becoming both the state's vice and venereal disease capital.

For years, prostitutes had plied their trade on the city's streets. But by the mid-1930s, their numbers had grown so large that they had little fear of arrest. "Macon is getting the unenviable reputation," said Ma, "for the offensive boldness of these immoral women." They were now openly soliciting men on some of the city's busiest streets:

> They loiter on Cherry Street, Third Street, Mulberry Street, Broadway and other prominent thoroughfares and they parade the sidewalks near hotels. Many tourists have been amazed at such shameless conduct and we do not intend to let such conditions exist any longer.[254]

Yet despite the "bold impudence" of these streetwalkers, the city council did little to abate the problem. Prostitution was one of the grim realities of life. Short of arresting every suspicious woman on the street, there was not much it could do.

Nevertheless, Ma and her fellow officers patrolled the streets for women she knew to be prostitutes. Beginning in September 1939, she went on night duty, working from eight o'clock in the evening into the early hours of the following morning. Much of her time was spent in the all-night establishments where enterprising women arranged assignations with men. But with no state or city statute making it a crime to solicit money for sex, she could only charge the women with loitering.[255]

A similar problem existed in the tourist camps and roadhouses in the county. While such places had to be licensed, they were subjected to little regulation, a fact that angered churches and residents in the areas where they were located. The tourist camps or motels were particularly offensive. Although advertised as lodging for travelers, they were used more often than not by locals looking for hookups with prostitutes.[256]

Citizens living in the Lynmore-Mikado section of the county became so enraged at the vice situation in the tourist camps and juke joints that they petitioned the Bibb County commissioners to deny licenses to establishments that tolerated vice. This was part of a larger vice crusade supported by the Mikado Baptist Brotherhood to rid their area of "undesirable jook joints and tourist camps." While the assistant solicitor admitted that vice was out of control in both the city and county, there had to be "tangible evidence to substantiate criminal charges against undesirable spots rather than hearsay and indignant generalized complaints."[257]

The *Macon News* was at the forefront of the fight and called on all citizens to join its "drive to clean up bawdry juke joints, tourist camps catering to illegitimate trade." It criticized those who attacked resorts like Rainbow Gardens, a recreational facility for Blacks that had a dance hall as well as a swimming pool, but ignored the more numerous White juke joints that operated beyond the rules of common decency. Citing the tourist camps as some of the most flagrant offenders, it declared that the camps were "actually places of assignation" that "will not rent cabins to tourists, as the turnover of unmarried couples is faster, hence more lucrative."[258]

The paper maintained that the city had "allowed White people to get away with things for which we put negroes under the jail." It added that the city had been far too lenient with the owners of tourist camps and clubs. "White folks' jooks, as well as negroes," said the paper, "must be cleaned up or closed up."[259]

To illustrate the impact of the juke joints on the city and county's young people, *Macon News* columnist Don Weldon wrote a story about a young girl by the name of Eileen Darby. Although a fictional character, she was a composite of many girls who worked the juke joints and tourist camps. Eileen was from a good family but left home at a young age to work in a juke joint. It was there that she fell under the influence of an unsavory crowd who spent most of their evenings listening to the "joy box" and downing shots of hard liquor. It was not long before she became enthralled with a local hoodlum named Leland Harvey. After several trysts with Harvey at a tourist camp, she became his partner in crime and wound up in jail.[260]

Weldon blamed city and county officials for licensing establishments that "willingly harbor criminals and their deluded young 'Mols.'" The dens of vice, he said, were profiting from the moral destruction of the area's young people. "They reap tens of thousands of dollars in profit each month— and every dirty dollar of it is a contribution to the future misery of some youngster headed hell-bent for a criminal career." It was time to act, he declared. "This column has time and time again called attention to the cheap joints operating in Macon and to the wide-open tourist camps which rent the same cottages five or six times in each 24 hours." He ended by demanding that "somebody in authority do something besides talk."[261]

Apparently, somebody had been listening in Atlanta. Macon, like other cities with military bases, was struggling to control prostitution and venereal disease. In March 1943, the state legislature passed a law that, according to Senator Everett Millican, one of the sponsors of the original bill, "hit at prostitution in all its forms and at all persons aiding prostitutes." Besides making solicitation for sex a crime, now "any person with knowledge or good reason to know of the intention of the lessee or rentee to use such place for prostitution" would be guilty of a misdemeanor for the first two offenses and a felony for the third. This section of the law targeted, said Millican, "any house, place, building, tourist camp, or other structure or trailer or other conveyance."[262]

In an effort to address the problem of pimps, cab drivers, bellhops and hotels that were arranging hookups for soldiers, the law was specific. Any persons who "cause, induce, persuade, encourage, or procure a woman to become or remain a prostitute, or receive any money or thing of value from a woman engaged in prostitution," read the statute, "will be guilty of a misdemeanor for the first offense and a felony for the second."[263]

The new law gave Macon authorities a much-needed tool that they could use to prosecute streetwalkers and those who aided and abetted them. As a result, during the war years, the police were booking one hundred girls per week for prostitution. Once charged, they were taken to the city stockade, where nurses from the VD clinic examined them. Those who tested positive

This army poster warned soldiers that their most dangerous enemies were in bars and saloons. *Courtesy of the Library of Congress.*

for syphilis were sent to a rapid treatment center near Gainesville, while those with gonorrhea were treated in Macon.[264]

Dr. Applewhite and Ma continued the battle against prostitution and venereal infection after the war. Although they had made significant strides in containing the problem, it persisted. In an interview with the *Telegraph* in 1949, Ma explained that two out of every ten streetwalkers arrested were infected—significantly less, said the VD clinic, than during the early 1940s.

Still frustrated with the amount of money spent on chain gangs and prison farms rather than schools to help lawbreakers and prostitutes, Ma said her department tried to work with girls as long as possible. Their goal was always to help them leave the profession and start a new life. She sincerely believed that they could eventually take their place in the world as respectable citizens. She ended by saying, "Some of the finest girls I know have been rescued from houses of prostitution."[265]

Chapter 14

A SCANDAL AND
AN UNSOLVED MURDER

One year before Ma McCord retired, many of Macon's citizens and officials began to question whether the city's police department was doing its all to stop gambling and prostitution in the city. In October 1953, the Bibb County Grand Jury found that the "problems of pinball machines have become greater than before in both city and county." This was a troubling development: "It is apparent that it encourages racketeering all the way to the ownership of the machines themselves up to and including the ownership of the places where the machines are located." It stated further that the police department appeared to have softened its investigation into prostitution in the city. Guest registers were not being checked thoroughly for lewd women who plied their trade in downtown hotels.[266]

While a later grand jury in 1956 commended the department for its efficiency and integrity, another in 1971 was not so convinced that the department was actually enforcing the law. "Drugs, prostitution, and gambling are 'big business' in Macon," said the jury. "These could not continue to flourish without the knowledge of some top law enforcement officials." To ensure that detectives not be "under prolonged pressure to accept payoffs," the jury recommended that "all members of the vice squad be changed every six months, as is the practice in most metropolitan areas, so their identity does not become known to law violators."[267]

According to the Macon *Telegraph*, the jurors were convinced that gambling and prostitution were operating freely under the noses of the police. This was evident when Billy Cecil Doolittle, co-owner of the Sportsman's Club on Third Street, was arrested in 1969 and 1970 on gambling charges. Doolittle's operation appeared to be relatively small, with only a few poker tables located in a back room. He paid a fine of $500 and was released.[268]

But from August to December 1970, the FBI launched a nationwide investigation into organized gambling. What it uncovered was that Doolittle had been running a sports betting outfit with direct ties to Las Vegas. Tellingly, Macon's police department was not informed of the raid.[269]

A few weeks after the grand jury's presentment, the police department made a raid on Welch's Jazz Lounge, a Black-owned club on Mulberry Street. The raid led to the arrest of Percy Welch, the owner, and forty-six others for prostitution. Mrs. Lovernall Jackson, Welch's mother-in-law, was one of those arrested. She, like her son-in-law, would be charged with operating a house of prostitution.[270]

Chief of Detectives W.H. Bargeron denied that the raid stemmed from the grand jury's findings. Since May, said the chief, the department had been using undercover detectives from Fort Valley to investigate the lounge. He maintained that the department could have snared many more in the prostitution ring had the grand jury not been so vocal in its criticisms.[271]

By the spring of 1973, members of the city council were coming to believe that something was not quite right in the city's police department. Aldermen Keith Stringfellow and Sydney Pyles called repeatedly for an inquiry into the detectives' bureau and the vice squad but were ignored by Mayor Ronnie Thompson and the other aldermen. "If you know something about the squad," said the mayor, "bring charges." Without evidence, the council, he insisted, should keep quiet.[272]

After federal agents and the Bibb County Sheriff's Office conducted one of the largest lottery raids in Macon's history that December, more members of the city council became suspicious. Why weren't the city's detectives and vice squad notified of the raid? When asked, Assistant U.S. Attorney Hale Almand said he "wouldn't want to comment because I don't know where we're going from here."[273]

By February 1974, the U.S. attorney's office had called a federal grand jury to investigate gambling and police corruption. Between March and April, federal agents seized over one hundred gambling machines, gambling records and $630 in a number of locations in Macon. W.N. "Dyke" Hawes, a well-known distributor of music and amusement machines in the city, was one of the many arrested and charged. Interestingly, Hawes had met with the mayor just a few days before the raids.[274]

Just prior to one of the last raids, Chief Bargeron entered the Macon Hospital complaining of chest pains. Soon after, he was found hanging in the bathroom of his room. He died twelve hours later. Hospital officials refused to disclose the cause of death.[275]

Was this suicide or homicide? The district attorney's office and Bibb County Coroner A.R. King Jr. immediately launched an investigation. With the assistance of a locksmith, the team was able to seize records from the chief's office safe. They also opened his bank safety deposit box in search of clues.[276]

There was hope, also, that the autopsy would provide a lead. But the autopsy was inconclusive. While the principal cause of death was cardiac arrest, said the coroner, he did not know the contributing causes. The investigation would continue.

When asked for his input, Mayor Thompson said he had not ruled out homicide. "There is a homicide possibility because of police investigations involving individuals possibly connected with organized crime." Believing that the district attorney's office was biased, he asked the Justice Department to look into Bargeron's death. "I want agents in here who are not politically oriented, who have not been prejudiced by printed and spoken rumor, hearsay, gossip, innuendo, and half-truths."[277]

W.H. Bargeron, Macon's chief of detectives in 1974, was found hanging in the bathroom of his Macon Hospital room soon after learning that federal agents had conducted raids on gambling establishments that were paying him and other officers protection money. *Courtesy of the* Macon News.

There would be a federal investigation but not into Bargeron's death. In May 1974, the U.S. attorney's office began indicting members of the police department, the detective's bureau and the vice squad for lying to the federal grand jury about accepting bribes.

The first was captain Ralph Gober, a traffic officer. Although suspended from the force by the chief of police, Gober, who had contributed to the campaigns of the mayor and members of the council, was soon reinstated. But it was not for long. In exchange for a five-month sentence for perjury, he admitted that he collected money from gambling houses and turned it over to Bargeron. He later testified that he had received fifty dollars per month to warn Martin Music Company when outside law enforcement planned to raid its gambling machine operations.[278]

There were more indictments to follow. B.C. Cranford, who had succeeded Bargeron as chief of detectives, together with vice squad detectives Robert L. Newsome, Lonnie M. Brown, James B. Finney and Julian Seymour Jr., would all stand trial for perjury and accepting bribes from gamblers, pimps and prostitutes. The trial, which began May 12, 1975, would be lengthy. The U.S. attorney had subpoenaed over two hundred witnesses to testify.[279]

Those who would take the stand represented a cross section of Macon's underworld: prostitutes, pimps, bookies, lottery operators and bootleggers. In explicit language, a string of prostitutes testified that they performed oral sex on the defendants so that they could stay in business. Some also spoke of seeing Detectives Lonnie Brown and Julian Seymour accept payoffs from prostitutes and pimps at the Brown House Motor Hotel. All the accused, said a number of nightclub owners, demanded payment if they wanted to keep their businesses open. James Hughes, who worked in William Prentice Tucker's gambling business and had operated a prostitution ring out of the Central Hotel in 1973, said he saw Tucker make regular protection payments to Seymour, Cranford and Brown.[280]

Hughes, who was in jail at the time of the trial for the murder of James Nash, was the government's key witness in its case against Tucker and two of his associates, Daisy Bell Hughes and Ronald Jackson, for violating federal and state gaming laws. Hughes described himself as a "flunky" in Tucker's million-dollar lottery operation, but his testimony revealed that he was intricately involved in the business. According to Hughes, Jackson would bring the daily receipts to Hughes's mobile home, where he and she would count the money and the tickets while Tucker watched. The operation was later moved to the Central Hotel. It was there that others involved in the lottery would bring their receipts to Tucker. Winning lottery numbers were obtained from the daily stock and bond market reports in the newspapers.[281]

Like Tucker, the owners of Martin Music Company, Star Music Company and Peach State Company would also stand trial for illegal gaming in 1975. Amusement machines seized in raids in 1974, said the government, were actually gambling devices that made cash payments to winning players. Based on the testimony of employees of the businesses, the owners made regular payments to the five detectives for protection.[282]

In a surprising turn of events, Shirley Ann Dixon, daughter of the late Thomas Talmadge Dixon, voluntarily came forward to testify against the indicted police officers. She said she felt it was important that the truth "should be out" about what she had seen during her childhood. Her father for a long while had conducted lottery and whiskey operations in the city and county, and he had financed Seymour in a distilling operation. She even said that she recalled that Seymour was present at a still with her and her father.[283]

But the most damaging testimony was yet to come. Her father, Shirley asserted, made payoffs to Bargeron, Cranford, Seymour and Finney once a month from 1959 to 1966. The corruption that officials had hoped was only a recent phenomenon was far deeper and more prolonged than they imagined.

Despite the overwhelming amount of evidence brought to the separate trials, all the defendants maintained their innocence. But the juries were not convinced and returned guilty verdicts. All, however, would appeal their convictions.

With the exception of B.C. Cranford, whose conviction was reversed by the U.S. Circuit Court after he suddenly died, the defendants would ultimately serve varying sentences for either racketeering or soliciting and accepting bribes and payoffs from vice operations. Julian E. Seymour Jr., who was connected to more of the bribes and payoffs than any other officer, would serve fifteen years in the federal penitentiary.[284]

But there were still unanswered questions. One, of course, was whether Bargeron had actually hanged himself. Many in the city were convinced that he knew too much and was murdered.

There was also the mysterious death on July 19, 1968, of LaSonjae Shockley, a dancer and waitress at the Scarlet Garter on Riverside Drive. It appeared, according to detectives, that someone had come through an open window and surprised her. A broken, bloody rolling pin was found near the body.[285]

Detective Julian Seymour Jr. was convicted of taking bribes from businessmen who ran lotteries and leased slot machines to gaming houses. *Courtesy of the Macon* Telegraph.

On closer inspection, the county medical examiner determined that she had not died from blunt-force trauma. More than likely, she was strangulated with the sheet found wrapped around her body. The head wounds she suffered were inflicted, he concluded, after she was dead. There was no evidence of sexual assault.

At first, detectives thought her ex-husband, Govan Shockley, might be responsible. He certainly had a motive. He admitted that he had not been happy with the fact that

LaSonjae was a regular performer at the Scarlet Garter and that she was having relationships with men old enough to be her father. He also suspected that she had been part of a prostitution ring.[286]

Vonnie Pitts, the roommate who found her, was also under suspicion. In January of the same year, she married Shockley. Whether or not LaSonjae and Govan had actually gotten a divorce before her murder is uncertain. Nevertheless, Vonnie and Govan maintained that they were husband and wife. This, however, did not keep Vonnie from admitting that LaSonjae was afraid of Shockley.[287]

LaSonjae's murder was never solved. But in light of the revelations about the ten-year history of corruption in the police department, some officials and investigative journalists believed that her death might in some way be connected to Macon's underworld. Whether it was remains a mystery.

Chapter 15

AN EVENING'S ENTERTAINMENT

*M*a McCord watched as the city's prostitutes explored new and creative ways to ply their trade. With no protected red-light district and most of the boardinghouses in the city shuttered, many retreated to the Brown House Motor Hotel, the Central Hotel, the Dempsey and the Macon Hotel. The Brown House, named for Macon's oldest and most illustrious hotel, developed an infamous reputation during the 1960s and '70s for being particularly accommodating to pimps and prostitutes.

According to John W. Nichols, an eighteen-year-old army specialist whose unit was assigned to guard the B-52s at Warner Robins Air Base in 1965, the Brown House was well known to young men seeking female entertainment. It was not unusual, said Nichols, for young soldiers to go in groups to the hotel. Once there, they would meet one of the bellhops, who would then take them to the fifth floor for their assignations. The typical fee was ten dollars.[288]

Later, many enterprising women who wanted to avoid detection purchased business licenses to establish modeling agencies. For example, Heaven's Best, also known as Middle Georgia Referrals Inc., was registered as a corporation with the Georgia secretary of state's office in 1982. Located in a building on Vineville Avenue owned by Marshall I. Flatau, a local real estate broker, the business advertised itself as a modeling service, offering both nude and lingerie modeling sessions. The Macon police were suspicious. Posing as potential clients, undercover officers contacted the service to arrange

The Brown House Motor Hotel located on Broadway was known in Macon and the surrounding towns as a secure place to have assignations with the city's prostitutes. *Courtesy of the Middle Georgia Archives, Washington Memorial Library.*

sessions with its models at a local motel. When the women arrived, they told the officers that they would provide sexual services for a price. They were promptly arrested and charged with solicitation.[289]

The *Macon News* also did some investigating of its own. A female reporter called the agency to inquire about a potential modeling job. A lady who identified herself as "J" asked if she had any modeling experience. The reporter said no. Apparently it made no difference. Later that evening, J called the reporter with a job offer for that evening. When the reporter again said she had no experience, J asked if she understood what was expected of her. She declined the offer.[290]

Further investigation led the reporter to a woman who had been working as a prostitute for the company. Most of the calls she got were for rendezvous with men in the early morning hours who had been drinking. Customers, she said, paid eighty dollars per hour plus tips. After the session, she would take the money, minus the tip, to the office. The agency got fifty dollars, while she got thirty.[291]

After the *News* published its front-page story connecting Heaven's Best to prostitution on February 6, 1982, Marshall Flatau became incensed and brought suit for libel. The story, he claimed, suggested that he knew before signing the lease that the business was just a front for a prostitution ring. As a result, he had been humiliated, and his business had suffered. He asked for $750 in damages. Flatau, however, failed to prove that he had been libeled. The story, it was decided, did not say he had been involved in anything illegal or immoral.[292]

Actually, the trial did more harm to Flatau's reputation than the story. Witnesses who worked in his office testified that everyone knew Middle Georgia Referrals sold sex rather than modeling sessions. Knowing that the prostitutes frequented the building at night, some said they were afraid to use the bathrooms for fear they might contract a venereal disease. Even Flatau's wife complained about the situation. One woman stated that she quit her job out of fear that the building would be raided.[293]

Things were not going so well for Heaven's Best by the spring of 1982. The arrest of several of its sex workers and the negative publicity stemming from the *Macon News'* story convinced its owners to pack up and leave town.[294]

Of course, there were still those who operated brothels out of their homes or worked the downtown streets. In May 1983, undercover police arrested

Marshall Realty, which owned this building, leased office space to Heaven's Best Modeling Agency. *Courtesy of the* Macon News.

three women for prostitution at the intersection of Poplar and Third Streets. The same evening, two men were arrested in Central City Park for soliciting sodomy. One was so bold as to jump into the car with the officer. Later, in the fall of 1984, Macon detectives raided a house on Napier Avenue. Two sisters, Debra Jean "Nana Sue" and Gloria Ann "Hootchie" Redding, were arrested for solicitation of sodomy.[295]

By the mid-1980s, prostitution was not, however, as rife in the city as it had been in earlier years. Most prostitutes worked street corners and a few clubs, said Major Terry Singleton. And the hotels and motels that once were the favorite haunts of sex traffickers were no more. "Prostitution here in Macon, if it exists at all, exists on a very small scale," said Police Chief Jim Brooks. One reason, he said, was that many of the prostitution busts were linked to illegal drugs. Instead of a misdemeanor, prostitutes now faced the possibility of a felony conviction.[296]

But for those who were cunning enough to disguise their operations, there was money to be made. After a yearlong investigation, in 1998, the vice and narcotics division of neighboring Warner Robins broke up a prostitution ring that was run out of a house in a quiet neighborhood in the city. According to police chief Dan Hart, it was a well-organized operation utilizing the latest technology. "They had a 1-800 number that ran through to another city. They'd call the girls and get them to go to the city where the caller was calling from." Although Carolyn and Stephen Holton, the owners of what they called Heather's Escort Service, did not actually use their home for sexual encounters, they were arrested and charged with keeping a house of prostitution and pimping.[297]

EPILOGUE

No doubt the police scandals that rocked the city in 1975 left Ma McCord heartbroken. She had loved and respected her fellow officers and devoted much of her life to doing what was best for the people of Macon. If she had ever been offered bribes, it's highly unlikely that she would have ever accepted them. On the contrary, even though her salary was meager, she never failed to use her own money to help the unfortunate who lived and worked in the city's underworld.

After twenty-six years of service, Ma retired from the police department in 1954. Having lost her husband of nearly thirty years in 1945, she later married C.L. McLeod. The couple, however, were only together for a few short years. Now twice widowed, Ma lived out her days on a shady, tree-lined street in West Macon teaching monogramming at the YWCA and doing charity work at the Vineville Presbyterian Church.

Reflecting on her career in interviews with the *Telegraph* and the *News*, Ma said Macon had been a "very wild place" during her years as the city's only policewoman.

> *The work then was quite different from what it is now. If I were doing now what I did then, the Supreme Court would put me under the jail. I was the only policewoman in Macon, so I had to do everything from searching people to investigating to arresting.*[298]

In the years following her retirement from the Macon police force, Ma McCord did charity work and taught monograming at the city YWCA. *Courtesy of the Macon* Telegraph.

Much of her work included helping those who couldn't help themselves. "In the early days I was there, there was no department of public welfare or social service, so people called the police department for help."[299]

She had seen the best and the worst of Macon, she said. And no doubt she had. In 1980, she died at the age of ninety and is buried next to her first husband in Riverside Cemetery.

DR. APPLEWHITE, WHO HAD struggled to contain the spread of venereal infections as well other diseases since his appointment as public health officer for Macon and Bibb County in 1926, decided to resign in 1944 and return to private practice. He continued to work closely with area hospitals and received numerous honors, including being named Practitioner of the Year by the Medical Association of Georgia in 1964 and Doctor of the Year by the staff of the Middle Georgia Hospital in 1966. He died in 1971 at the age of eighty and, like Ma, is buried in Riverside Cemetery.

Camp Wheeler, the army facility that Dr. Applewhite had worked so hard to protect from venereal disease, continued as an active training camp until its decommissioning in 1945. With a troop capacity of close to 26,000, the camp played a critical role in the war effort. During the course of its operation, it's estimated that 218,000 soldiers were trained at Camp Wheeler.

Many of the ministers who crusaded against alcohol, prostitution and gambling in Macon during the early years of the century had died, moved from the city or left the pulpit by World War II. Although retired, Dr. W.N. Ainsworth continued his fight against alcohol, demanding in 1941 that the state legislature enact a new prohibition law. However, in 1942, the former president of Wesleyan College, pastor of Mulberry Street Methodist Church and bishop of the Methodist synod died at the age of seventy while visiting his son in Asheville, North Carolina. He, too, is buried in Riverside Cemetery.

It's probable that Dr. Ainsworth and other veterans of the fight against gambling and alcohol would be appalled to learn that the people of Georgia voted to implement a lottery in the 1990s, thus making legal the vice that had been so much a part of Macon's underworld. They would also be horrified to know that the city not only has a multitude of bars and liquor stores but that they, as well as restaurants, would also be permitted to sell alcohol on Sundays.

Tybee, the community that had long served as both the city's official and unofficial vice district for much of its history, maintained its infamous reputation after the houses of ill fame were closed. Juke joints and shot houses, offering patrons a bit of moonshine whiskey for a nominal price, still operated in the district with little interference from authorities. And prostitutes, unable to find accommodations elsewhere, found a boardinghouse or two that would rent to them in the neighborhood.

Although considered an impoverished and crime-infested area, the community had churches, a few small stores and lunch rooms and a theater. By the 1950s, manufacturing companies like Procter & Gamble, Dixie Bag Company, Acme Brewing Company, Birdsey Flour Mill, Triangle Chemical Company and the Central of Georgia Railroad had also made the district their headquarters.[300]

The Roxy Theatre was particularly important to Tybee's people. They could not attend the Whites-only theaters, but at the Roxy, they could at

Most of the people who lived in Tybee still rented their houses from White businessmen. Many of the structures had no indoor plumbing or electricity even as late as the 1950s. *Courtesy of the Macon* Telegraph *and the Washington Memorial Library Archives.*

By the early 1960s, Macon city officials saw Tybee as a blighted area and a health hazard. Eventually, the houses would be torn down, leaving residents to find housing in other areas of the city. *Courtesy of the Macon* Telegraph *and the Washington Memorial Library Archives.*

The Roxy Theater was a source of pride to the people of Tybee in the 1950s and '60s, providing residents (who were barred from Macon's "Whites only" theaters) with opportunities to see the latest movies as well as musical performances. *Courtesy of Historic Macon Foundation.*

least see the latest movies on the big screen and hear Otis Redding, James Brown and Little Richard perform. It, like the community they had created southwest of the tracks, was a place all their own.

But city officials saw things differently. Tybee, in their view, was a blighted area of seven hundred one- and two-room shacks with no running water or electricity. And with irresponsible owners refusing to do repairs or upgrades to their property, the city decided to condemn the houses. Although residents made appeals to the city to save their community, there was little they could do.[301]

By the early 1970s, most of Tybee's residents had been forced to leave. Some scattered into other Black neighborhoods. Others went into public housing. Today, all that remains of the place that Macon's underworld once called home are brownfields, a few warehouses, scrapyards and ghosts.

NOTES

Introduction: Out of the Shadows

1. *Maloney's 1900 Macon, Georgia City Directory*. See also Iobst, *Civil War Macon*.
2. R.L. Polk & Co., *1905 Macon City Directory*.
3. Ibid.
4. Ibid.
5. Ibid.; *Sholes' Directory of the City of Macon*.

Chapter 1: No Rest for the Wicked

6. See Taylor, *Eating, Drinking, and Visiting*, and Rorabaugh, *Alcoholic Republic*.
7. Ibid.
8. Ayers, *Promise*, 173–82.
9. See Okrent, *Last Call*.
10. *Macon News*, July 29, 1907.
11. *Atlanta Journal*, September 24, 1906.
12. Macon *Telegraph*, December 30, 1907.
13. *Macon News*, November 7, 1907.
14. Macon *Telegraph*, May 11, 1911.
15. *Macon News*, January 22, 1913; Macon *Telegraph*, December 10, 1913.
16. Ibid.

17. Macon City Council minutes, April 18, 1911; *Macon News*, April 19, 1911.
18. Ibid.
19. *Macon News*, December 9, 1914.
20. *Macon News*, November 3, 1913.
21. *Macon News*, November 4, 1913.
22. *Macon News*, February 26, 1916.
23. *Macon News*, February 15, 1916.
24. Ibid.
25. *Macon News*, February 16, 1916.
26. Ibid.
27. *Macon News*, February 19, 1916.
28. Macon *Telegraph*, September 7, 1903.
29. *Macon News*, January 25, 1904.
30. *Macon News*, March 23, 1905.
31. Macon *Telegraph*, April 2, 1905.
32. *Macon News*, May 8, 1905.
33. Ibid.
34. Macon *Telegraph*, January 7, 1914.
35. Macon *Telegraph*, August 29, 1919.
36. Macon *Telegraph*, June 22, 1919.
37. Ibid.
38. Macon *Telegraph*, June 20, 1919.
39. Macon *Telegraph*, January 15, 1916.
40. Macon *Telegraph*, June 23, 1919.
41. Macon *Telegraph*, June 24, 1919.
42. Macon *Telegraph*, September 13, 1920.
43. Ibid.
44. Ibid.
45. Rosen, *Lost Sisterhood*, 112–35. See also Keire, *For Business & Pleasure*.
46. *Macon News*, April 22, 1901.
47. *Macon News*, June 23, 1911.
48. *Macon News*, May 24, 1913.
49. Macon *Telegraph*, January 14, 1915.
50. Macon *Telegraph*, October 2, 1912.
51. Elliot, *Social Evil*.
52. Ibid.
53. *Official Code of the City of Macon*, 1914.
54. See Macon City Council minutes for the years 1905–10.

Chapter 2: A Babylon Beyond the Tracks

55. Macon City Council Minutes, January 31, 1905.
56. R.L. Polk & Co., *1905 Macon City Directory.*
57. Ibid.
58. R.L. Polk & Co., *1915 Macon City Directory*.
59. *Macon News*, March 14, 1913.
60. *Official Code of the City of Macon 1914*, section 1096, 444.
61. *Macon Telegraph*, January 4, 1912, and April 24, 1913; *Macon News*, August 7, 1913, and January 17, 1914.
62. *Atlanta Constitution*, February 16, 1915; Macon *Telegraph*, February 15, 1915. For information regarding how American cities regulated their vice districts, see Keire, *For Business & Pleasure*.
63. *Macon News*, April 22, 1912; Macon *Telegraph*, March 11, 1913; October 16, 1912; and March 24, 1913.
64. Macon *Telegraph*, November 6, 1913.
65. *Macon News*, April 12, 1912.
66. Macon *Telegraph*, November 24, 1912.
67. Ibid.
68. Macon *Telegraph*, April 23, 1912, and February 3, 1913; *Macon News*, February 7, 1913, and April 7, 1913.

Chapter 3: By Persons Unknown

69. Macon *Telegraph*, March 9, 1913.
70. Macon *Telegraph*, December 25, 1914, and December 30, 1914; *Macon News*, January 1, 1915.
71. Macon *Telegraph*, February 4, 1912.
72. Ibid.
73. Macon *Telegraph*, February 5, 1912.
74. Macon *Telegraph*, November 3, 1919.
75. Macon *Telegraph*, July 31, 1922.
76. Ibid.
77. Ibid.
78. *Macon News*, September 25, 1922.
79. Ibid.

Chapter 4: A Fly in the Ointment

80. *Macon News*, March 31, 1913.
81. Ibid.
82. *Macon News*, August 17, 1913
83. Macon *Telegraph*, March 17, 1915.
84. Ibid.
85. Macon *Telegraph*, March 22, 1915.
86. Macon *Telegraph*, June 12, 1913. Roy Binion took money he was given to purchases groceries and went straight to Tybee. His father had him arrested.
87. Ibid.
88. Macon *Telegraph*, March 31, 1915.
89. Ibid.
90. Ibid.

Chapter 5: The Houses in Our Midst

91. Bederman, "Women Have Had Charge," 432–65.
92. *Atlanta Journal*, July 9, 1912.
93. *Atlanta Constitution*, June 29, 1912.
94. *Atlanta Georgian*, November 7, 1912, and November 14, 1912.
95. *Atlanta Journal*, December 29, 1913.
96. Ibid.
97. *Atlanta Journal*, September 26, 1912.
98. *Atlanta Journal*, June 9, 1913; *Atlanta Constitution*, June 7, 1914.
99. Ibid.
100. *Atlanta Georgian*, June 6, 1913; *Atlanta Constitution*, January 21, 1914.
101. *Atlanta Constitution*, December 5, 1915; Macon *Telegraph*, August 1, 1915.
102. *Atlanta Journal*, May 25, 1915.
103. *Atlanta Constitution*, August 2, 1915; August 4, 1915; and August 11, 1915.
104. *Atlanta Constitution*, October 15, 1915, and December 28, 1915.

Chapter 6: Fit to Fight

105. Lowry, *Soldiers Wouldn't Tell*, 104.
106. Catherine Clinton, "'Public Women' and Sexual Politics during the American Civil War," in Clinton and Silber, *Battle Scars*, 63.

107. Lowry, *Soldiers Wouldn't Tell*, 99–108.

108. Brandt, *No Magic Bullet*, 12–13.

109. Ibid., 40.

110. Ibid.; Parascandola, *Sex, Sin, Science*, 22. See also Allen, *Wages of Sin*.

111. *Macon News*, August 16, 1917.

112. Macon *Telegraph*, June 3, 1917.

113. Ibid.

114. Ibid.

115. *Macon News*, August 16, 1917.

116. Macon *Telegraph*, October 27, 1917; *Macon News*, November 19, 1917.

117. *Macon News*, October 25, 1917.

118. Ibid.

119. Ibid.

120. Ibid.

121. *Macon News*, October 26, 1917; Macon *Telegraph*, October 27, 1917.

122. Ibid.

123. Macon *Telegraph*, October 23, 1917.

124. Ibid.

125. Macon *Telegraph*, October 27, 1917.

Chapter 7: An Impromptu Underworld

126. *Macon News*, January 18, 1919.

127. Ibid.

128. Macon *Telegraph*, January 18, 1919.

129. Macon *Telegraph*, January 21, 1919.

130. *Macon News*, January 20, 1919.

131. Macon *Telegraph*, January 17, 1920.

132. *Macon News*, February 4, 1916; February 9, 1919; and December 7, 1923; Macon *Telegraph*, May 3, 1926.

133. Macon *Telegraph*, January 14, 1922; March 29, 1922; July 8, 1922; and July 22, 1924; *Macon News*, February 8, 1924.

134. *Macon News*, November 19, 1922.

135. *Macon News*, May 20, 1925.

Chapter 8: Murder and Whiskey on Swift Creek Road

136. Macon *Telegraph*, July 14, 1926.
137. Ibid.
138. Ibid.
139. Macon *Telegraph*, July 13, 1926.
140. Ibid.
141. Ibid.
142. Ibid.
143. *Macon News*, October 4, 1926.
144. Macon *Telegraph*, July 17, 1926.
145. Ibid.
146. Macon *Telegraph*, July 28, 1926; *Macon News*, August 31, 1926.
147. Macon *Telegraph*, July 28, 1926.
148. Ibid.
149. Ibid.
150. Ibid.
151. Macon *Telegraph*, July 19, 1926.
152. *Macon News*, August 31, 1926.
153. Macon *Telegraph*, September 5, 1926.
154. Macon *Telegraph*, September 19, 1926.
155. Ibid.

Chapter 9: A Call to Arms

156. Macon *Telegraph*, July 19, 1926.
157. Ibid.
158. Ibid.
159. Ibid.
160. Ibid.
161. Macon *Telegraph*, July 24, 1926.
162. Ibid.
163. Ibid.
164. Ibid.
165. *Macon News*, July 26, 1926.
166. *Macon News*, July 24, 1926, and July 27, 1926.
167. *Macon News*, July 20, 1926.
168. Macon *Telegraph*, August 9, 1926.

169. Ibid.

170. Ibid.

171. Macon *Telegraph*, August 11, 1926.

172. Ibid.

173. Macon *Telegraph*, August 9, 1926.

174. *Macon News*, September 11, 1926

175. Ibid.

Chapter 10: The Fever

176. Macon *Telegraph*, October 1, 1922.

177. Ibid.

178. Macon *Telegraph*, September 8, 1928.

179. *Macon News*, September 22, 1933.

180. Ibid.

181. *Macon News*, October 29, 1934.

182. Ibid.

183. *Macon News*, November 26, 1934.

184. Macon *Telegraph*, January 14, 1935.

185. Ibid.

186. Macon *Telegraph*, December 8, 1935.

187. Macon *Telegraph*, May 18, 1936.

188. Ibid.

189. Ibid.

190. Ibid.

191. *Macon News*, October 24, 1941.

192. Ibid.

193. Ibid.

194. *Macon News*, October 25, 1941.

195. *Macon News*, October 30, 1941.

196. *Macon News*, December 2, 1941.

Chapter 11: Put 'Em Where They Belong

197. Macon *Telegraph*, November 15, 1980.

198. *Macon News*, June 17, 1930.

199. Ibid.

200. Macon *Telegraph*, April 18, 1928.
201. Ibid.
202. Ibid.
203. *Macon News*, February 23, 1974.
204. Ibid.
205. Ibid.
206. Macon *Telegraph*, September 18, 1949.
207. Ibid.
208. Ibid.
209. Ibid.
210. Ibid.
211. *Macon News*, April 3, 1935.
212. Ibid.
213. Ibid.
214. Ibid.
215. Ibid.
216. *Macon News*, May 1, 1935.
217. Macon *Telegraph*, May 5, 1935.
218. Macon *Telegraph*, May 3, 1935.
219. Macon *Telegraph*, May 18, 1935.
220. *Macon News*, May 12, 1937; Macon *Telegraph*, May 13, 1937.
221. Macon *Telegraph*, May 12, 1937, and May 16, 1937.
222. Macon *Telegraph*, May 13, 1937.
223. Ibid.
224. Macon *Telegraph*, September 7, 1937.
225. *Macon News*, May 13, 1937.
226. Macon *Telegraph*, May 21, 1937.
227. Ibid.
228. Ibid.
229. Ibid.
230. Macon *Telegraph*, May 13, 1937.
231. *Macon News*, March 26, 1938.
232. *Macon News*, February 2, 1938.

Chapter 12: Dr. Applewhite's War

233. *Macon News*, August 15, 1940.
234. Ibid.

235. *Macon News*, December 14, 1940.

236. Macon *Telegraph*, October 2, 1941.

237. *Macon News*, October 2, 1941.

238. Macon *Telegraph*, October 24, 1941.

239. Macon *Telegraph*, October 7, 1941.

240. Ibid.

241. Ibid.; *Macon News*, October 9, 1941, and October 10, 1941.

242. *Macon News*, October 13, 1941.

243. *Macon News*, October 14, 1941.

244. *Macon News*, October 16, 1941.

245. *Macon News*, October 23, 1941.

246. Ibid.

247. Ibid.

248. Macon *Telegraph*, October 24, 1941.

249. Ibid.

250. Ibid.

251. Ibid.

252. Ibid.

253. *Macon News*, December 27, 1941.

Chapter 13: Streetwalkers and Juke Joint Snipers

254. *Macon News*, February 27, 1936.

255. *Macon News*, September 14, 1939.

256. *Macon News*, November 29, 1937.

257. Ibid.

258. *Macon News*, July 19, 1940.

259. Ibid.

260. *Macon News*, May 12, 1943.

261. Ibid.

262. Ibid.

263. *Macon News*, March 18, 1943.

264. Macon *Telegraph*, October 13, 1949.

265. Ibid.

Chapter 14: A Scandal and an Unsolved Murder

266. Macon *Telegraph*, July 17, 1915.
267. Ibid.
268. Ibid.
269. Ibid.
270. *Macon News*, October 11, 1971.
271. Macon *Telegraph*, March 5, 1973.
272. Ibid.
273. Ibid.
274. Macon *Telegraph*, September 6, 1974.
275. *Macon News*, April 20, 1914.
276. Ibid.
277. Macon *Telegraph*, April 23, 1974.
278. Macon *Telegraph*, September 9, 1974.
279. Macon *Telegraph*, May 12, 1975.
280. Ibid.
281. *Macon News*, January 21, 1975.
282. Macon *Telegraph*, January 23, 1975.
283. *Macon News*, May 14, 1975.
284. *Macon News*, May 20, 1975, and May 31, 1975.
285. Macon *Telegraph*, February 8, 1969.
286. Ibid.
287. Ibid.

Chapter 15: An Evening's Entertainment

288. Interview with John Nichols, March 30, 2024.
289. *Macon News*, February 16, 1982, and December 1, 1982.
290. Ibid.
291. Ibid.
292. *Macon News*, November 30, 1982.
293. Ibid.
294. Macon *Telegraph*, January 2, 1983.
295. Macon *Telegraph*, May 12, 1983, and November 19, 1984.
296. Macon *Telegraph*, May 21, 1984.
297. Macon *Telegraph*, August 14, 1998.

Epilogue

298. *Macon News*, January 6, 1969.
299. Ibid.
300. Macon *Telegraph*, February 27, 2005.
301. Ibid.

BIBLIOGRAPHY

Newspapers

Atlanta Constitution
Atlanta Georgian
Atlanta Journal
Macon News
Macon *Telegraph*

Government Documents and City Directories

Macon City Council Minutes, 1900–1940.
Maloney's 1900 Macon Directory. Vol. 11. Atlanta, GA.
The Official City Code of Macon, Georgia, 1914.
R.L. Polk & Co. *1905 Macon City Directory*. Vol. 3. Birmingham, AL.
————. *1915 Macon City Directory*. Vol. 11. Birmingham, AL.
Sholes' Directory of the City of Macon, 1880. Vol. 2.

Books and Articles

Allen, Peter Lewis. *The Wages of Sin: Sex and Disease, Past and Present*. Chicago: University of Chicago Press, 2000.

Ayers, Edward L. *The Promise of the New South: Life After Reconstruction*. New York: Oxford University Press, 1991.

Bederman, Gail. "'The Women Have Had Charge of the Church Work Long Enough': The Men and Religion Forward Movement of 1911–1912 and the Masculinization of Protestantism." *American Quarterly* 41, no. 3 (September 1989): 432–65.

Brandt, Allan M. *No Magic Bullet: A Social History of Venereal Disease in the United States Since 1880*. New York: Oxford University Press, 1987.

Brundage, W. Fitzhugh. *Lynching in the South: Georgia and Virginia, 1880–1930*. Urbana: University of Illinois Press, 1995.

Clinton, Catherine, and Nina Silber, eds. *Battle Scars: Gender and Sexuality in the American Civil War*. New York: Oxford University Press, 2006.

Elliot, Albert W. *The Cause of the Social Evil and the Remedy*. Atlanta: Webb and Vary Printers, 1914.

Iobst, Richard. *Civil War Macon: The History of a Confederate City*. Macon: Mercer University Press, 1999.

Keire, Mara. *For Business & Pleasure: Red-Light Districts and the Regulation of Vice in the United States, 1890–1933*. Baltimore, MD: Johns Hopkins Press, 2010.

Lowry, Thomas P., MD. *The Story the Soldiers Wouldn't Tell: Sex and the Civil War*. Mechanicsburg, PA: Stackpole Books, 1994.

Okrent, Daniel. *Last Call: The Rise and Fall of Prohibition*. New York: Scribner, 2011.

Parascandola, John. *Sex, Sin, and Science: A History of Syphilis in America*. Westport, CT: Praeger, 2008.

Rorabaugh, W.J. *The Alcoholic Republic: An American Tradition*. New York: Oxford University Press, 1981.

Rosen, Ruth. *The Lost Sisterhood: Prostitution in America, 1900–1918*. Baltimore, MD: Johns Hopkins Press, 1982.

Taylor, Joe Gray. *Eating, Drinking, and Visiting in the South: An Informal History*. Baton Rouge: LSU Press, 1982.

INDEX

ABOUT THE AUTHOR

*P*hillip Andrew Gibbs is professor emeritus of history at Middle Georgia State University. Although a native Virginian, he has lived and taught in Georgia since 1987. An avid tennis player, cyclist and traveler, he also works as a professional musician, performing regularly throughout the southeastern United States with the Georgia Chryslers, a rock, pop and R&B band. He lives in Kathleen, Georgia, with his wife, Penny; their dog, Jack; and Moe the three-legged cat. This is his second book with The History Press.